Margaret M. Johnson's
Delicious IRELAND

JOHNNIE FOX'S PUB, Glencullen, Co. Dublin, Andikdublin/Fáilte Ireland

Alexa Kay Ondrush

Margaret M. Johnson's
Delicious IRELAND

Forty Years of Fabulous Food

Ambassador International
Greenville, South Carolina & Belfast, Northern Ireland

www.ambassador-international.com

Delicious Ireland

© 2024 by Margaret M. Johnson
All Rights Reserved

ISBN: 978-1-64960-514-6
E-ISBN: 978-1-64960-557-3

Cover photos: (top, left to right): THREE-CHEESE RÖSTI, *Bord Bia (Irish Food Board)*; SMOKED SALMON, *Kuvona / Dreamstime*; IRISH BREADS, *Margaret M. Johnson*.
(Main): IRISH WATERS' COD, POTATO & CELERIAC BOXTY, PRAWN BISQUE, SWEET POTATO & SHALLOT SALAD, *Jitka Smolkova / The Winding Stair, Dublin*

Back cover photos: (left to right): MACROOM BUFFALO FARM, Co. Cork; RICOTTA & TOMATO TART, The Winding Stair, Dublin; PHILIP HARRINGTON BUTCHER SHOP, Clonakilty, Co. Cork.
All photos *Margaret M. Johnson*

Montage design by Renée Johnson and Margaret M. Johnson

Edited by Katie Cruice Smith
Ebook conversion by Anna Riebe Raats
Cover and interior layout by Karen Slayne

AMBASSADOR INTERNATIONAL
Emerald House
411 University Ridge, Suite B14
Greenville, SC 29601, USA
www.ambassador-international.com

AMBASSADOR BOOKS
The Mount
2 Woodstock Link
Belfast, BT6 8DD, Northern Ireland, UK
www.ambassadormedia.co.uk

The colophon is a trademark of Ambassador.

DEDICATION

For the farmers and fisherman,

bakers and beekeepers,

brewers and distillers,

smokers and cheesemakers,

food producers and grocers,

chefs and restaurateurs,

cooks and cookery writers,

and all who continue to keep Irish food

as delicious as any on the planet.

MATT THE MILLER'S PUB & RESTAURANT, Kilkenny, Margaret M. Johnson

CONTENTS

INTRODUCTION　　　　　　　　　　　13

Chapter One
STARTERS　　　　　　　　　　　16
Soups, Salads, & Small Bites

Chapter Two
MAINS　　　　　　　　　　　51
Meat, Fish, Poultry, & Vegetarian Entrées

Chapter Three
SIDES　　　　　　　　　　　75
Mash & More

Chapter Four
SWEETS　　　　　　　　　　　93
Puddings, Tarts, Crumbles, & Cakes

ROSS CASTLE, Killarney, Patryk Kosminder/Dreamstime

GUINNESS
for Strength

The Village Inn

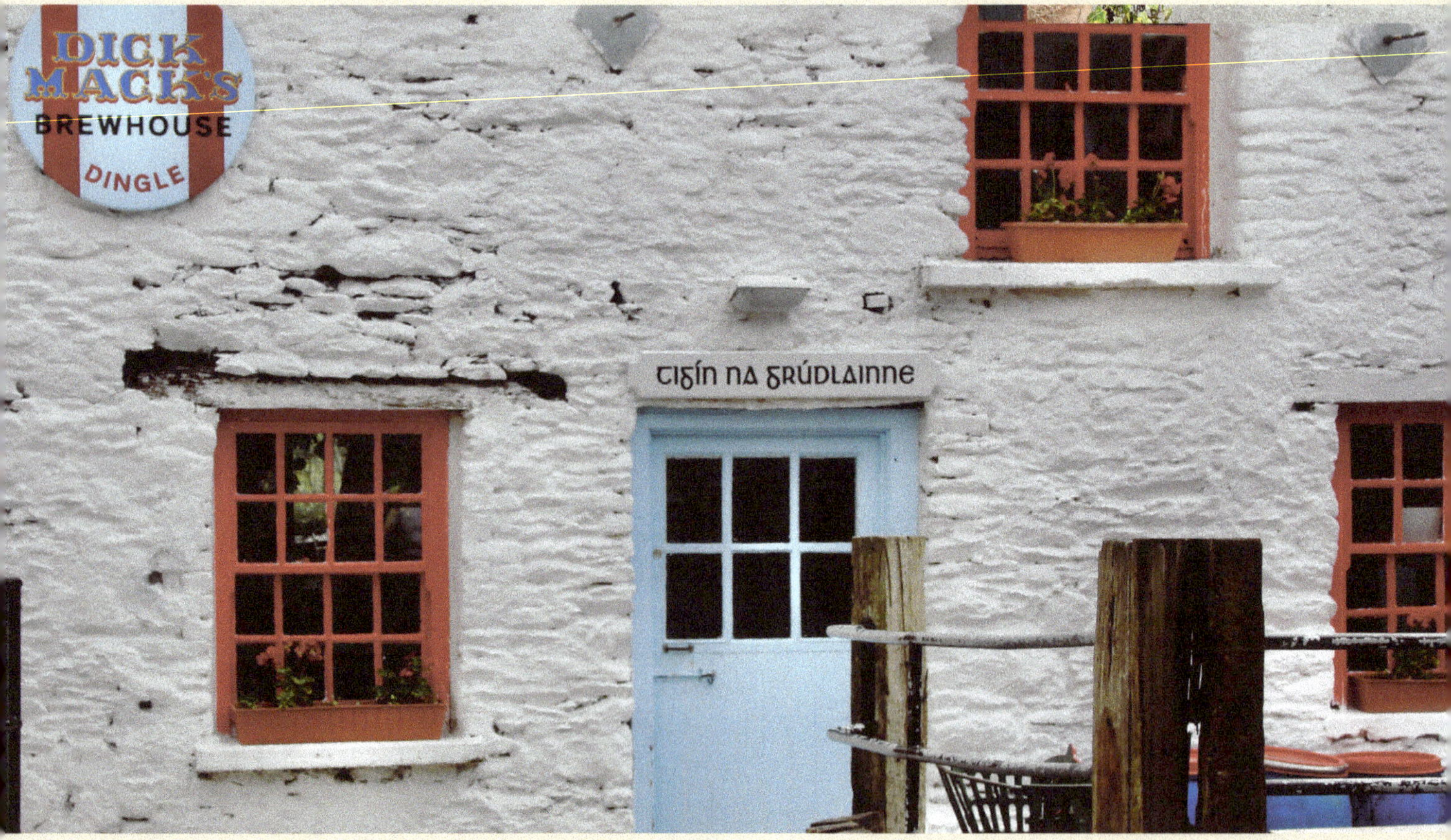
DICK MACK'S
BREWHOUSE
DINGLE
Tigín na Grúdlainne

Kirwan's Lane
THE HEART OF MEDIEVAL GALWAY
Handmade Arts and Crafts

KILKENNY CASTLE
ST CANICES CATHEDRAL
KILKENNY COURT HOUSE

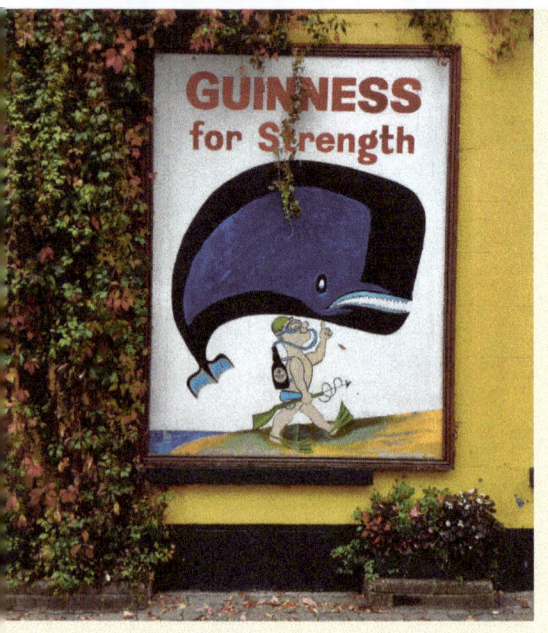

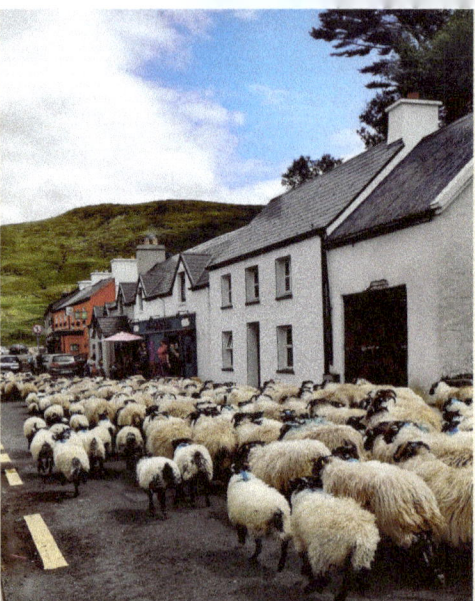

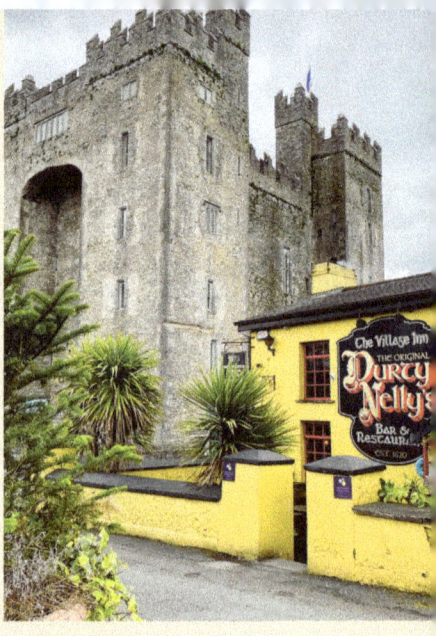

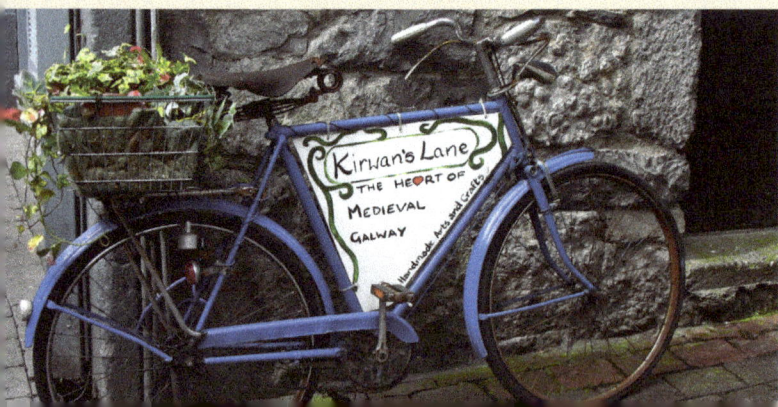

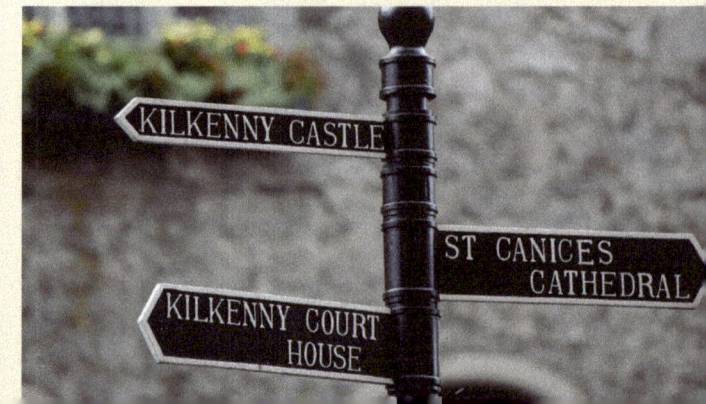

INTRODUCTION

There is no sincerer love than the love of food.
—George Bernard Shaw, Irish playwright

When I first visited Ireland in 1984, I began a love affair with the place where my grandparents and great-grandparents were born. I loved the people, the landscape, the history, the folklore, and the music. I have to admit, though, the affection didn't extend to my palate.

My children, ages seven and nine at the time, were enchanted by the woolly sheep and languid cows that slowed traffic on country lanes and brushed by our car close enough to touch. They were thrilled by the carnival atmosphere of Kerry's ancient Puck Fair in Killorglin with its bumper cars and carousel rides. But most grand was the big goat, in whose honor the fair is held, perched high above the square. My husband developed an insatiable appetite for the golf courses of the West of Ireland—Ballybunion, Lahinch, Waterville—and for pints of Guinness at pubs named Donahoe's, McCarthy's, and Hennessy's. We all treasured Ireland for reasons of our own; but none of us thought much about the food—except breakfast, perhaps, when we would sit down with total strangers and be fussed over about how we wanted our eggs cooked and whether we wanted a bit of porridge to start or needed more toast and jam.

To be honest, when you travel to a foreign country with young children, you look more for golden arches than for Michelin stars, so our 1984 visit to Ireland was not exactly a gourmet tour. We ate simple foods like Irish stew, fish and chips, and toasted sandwiches made with thick slabs of ham and slices of cheddar cheese; and we still came home raving about all things Irish. Serious food was irrelevant.

For years after that first trip, a day never passed when I didn't think of Ireland. Thanks to my Irish-born grandmother, I eventually had my name registered in the Foreign Births Record and was issued an Irish passport. I've traveled there more than six dozen times in the last forty years, and with each new visit, I've grown to love Ireland more—the people, the landscape, the history, the folklore, the music, and, finally, the food. I like to think of it as an "acquired taste."

Opposite page (top, left to right): KINSALE, Co. Cork, Margaret M. Johnson; LEENAUN, Co. Galway, Chloe Bolger/The Purple Door Café; BUNRATTY, Co. Clare, Margaret M. Johnson; (middle) DINGLE, Co. Kerry, Margaret M. Johnson; (bottom, left to right) GALWAY, Margaret M. Johnson; KILKENNY, Brian Morrison/Tourism Ireland

Tuesday Lunch.

Soupe au Pistou. — 3.50 / 5.50

Pepper Pot Soup — 3.75 / 5.75

Mussel + Smoked Fish Chowder — 3.75 / 5.

Crab Cakes w/ Piquant Mayo — 4.75 / 6.

Cherry Tomato + Goat's Cheese Pizza. — 6.9

Emmenthal + Asparagus Tart — 5.75.

Chicken Confit w/ Wild Rice + Puy Lentil Risotto

Roast Smoked Ham w/ Sage + Mustard Mash — 8.

Spiced Lamb Patties w/ Chargrilled Ratatouille — 8.

Chargrilled Tuna Steak Club Sandwich — 10

DUBLIN, Margaret M. Johnson

Pecan Pie

Over the course of forty years, food fairs, festivals, and farmers markets have blossomed; gourmet food shops have flourished; artisan cheesemakers have multiplied; and the number of Michelin-starred restaurants has grown to twenty-one. Farms are opening for tours to show visitors where real Irish food comes from; and restaurants promote indigenous ingredients on their menus, letting you know who raised the duck, smoked the salmon, and made the cheese.

Today, people are buzzing about Irish food, reveling in the modern, inspired, and cosmopolitan direction it's taken—from fine-dining restaurants to gastropubs, wine bars, and gourmet markets. In 1968, Irish food writer Theodora FitzGibbons declared, "The best food of a country is the traditional food which has been tried and tested over the centuries. It's food that suits the climate and uses the best products of that country; it's part of its history and civilization, and, ideally, the past and the present should be combined so that traditional food is not lost under a pile of tins or packages."

Delicious Ireland will show you how the food of Ireland—often used in Irish literature to provide focus, punctuation, and rhythm—has evolved over the past forty years. Think fresh mozzarella, ricotta, and halloumi cheese being made from milking buffalos raised on farms in County Cork; shiitake, oyster, and maitake mushrooms being cultivated in County Offaly; heritage, elephant, and black garlic being grown on farms in Counties Louth, Cork, and Kildare. As James Joyce once wrote, Ireland is no longer "outcast from life's feast."

With more than sixty inspired and innovative recipes—tasty starters like blue cheese and fig tartine; hearty mains like lamb with honey-apricot-tarragon sauce; inventive vegan and vegetarian options, such as butternut squash and leek tart; yummy potato cakes and gratins; decadent desserts ranging from timeless puddings to fruity crumbles; and great Irish cheeses to finish your meal—*Delicious Ireland* guides you on a decades-long culinary and photographic odyssey around the Emerald Isle and offers new experiences and fresh perspectives on Irish cuisine.

Bain taitneamh as do bhéile!
Bon appétit.

CHAPTER 1

STARTERS
Soups, Salads, & Small Bites

Cooking comes down to a sort of alchemy, its results an elixir, for suddenly here on one's table for family and friends is a new delicious concoction, a pleasure for everyone.
Myrtle Allen, *Cooking at Ballymaloe House*[1]

Potato & Celeriac Soup	19
Steamed Irish Mussels in Cider Cream	20
Root Vegetable & Red Lentil Soup	23
Lamb Croquettes	24
Creamy Mint Sauce	25
Kinsale Brown Soda Bread	27
Guinness & Malt Wheaten Bread	28
Walnut & Treacle Bread	29

Savol67/Dreamstime

---

1   Myrtle Allen, *Myrtle Allen's Cooking at Ballymaloe House: Featuring 100 Recipes from Ireland's Most Famous Guest House* (New York: Stewart, Tabori & Chang, Inc, 1990).

Cashel Blue Tartine with Roasted Figs & Prosciutto	30
Walnut Vinaigrette	31
Wild Mushroom & Ricotta Toast	33
Goat Cheese Tarts with Red Onion Marmalade	34
Goat Cheese & Tomato Charlottes	36
Roasted Beetroot & Citrus Salad with Cashel Blue Cheese	38
Citrus Dressing	39
Warm Mushroom & Black Pudding Salad	40
Wholegrain Mustard Vinaigrette	41
Hot Smoked Salmon Chowder	43
Chilli-smoked Salmon Fritters	44
Sweet Chilli Lime Sauce	45
Celeriac & Apple Remoulade	45
The Smokehouse	47

Martin Turzak/Dreamstime

POTATO & CELERIAC SOUP

Serves 4 to 6

LEEK and potato soup, also known as *brotchán foltchep* (from the Irish words meaning "broth" and "leeks"), is one of Ireland's most traditional soups. Once thickened with oatmeal, this "broth" is now thickened with potatoes and, more recently, celeriac. The root of a celery plant, celeriac has an earthy taste with a slight hint of celery and a texture close to that of turnip or parsnip. The soup is delicious served with buttered slices of one of the brown breads on pages 27, 28, and 29.

- 2 tablespoons butter
- 1 medium onion, chopped
- 2 large leeks (white and light green parts only), sliced
- 1 small celeriac, peeled and chopped
- 6 medium potatoes, peeled and cut into 1 1/2-inch pieces
- 1/2 teaspoon fresh thyme
- 6 cups canned low-sodium chicken broth
- 1 1/4 cups half and half
- Salt
- White pepper
- 2 tablespoons chopped fresh flat-leaf parsley
- Celery leaves or chopped fresh chives, for garnish

1. In large saucepan over medium heat, melt the butter. Add the onion, leeks, celeriac, and potatoes; stir to coat. Cook, stirring frequently, for 5 to 7 minutes, or until the vegetables are soft but not browned; stir in the thyme.
2. Add the broth; bring to a boil. Reduce heat to low. Cook, covered, for about 30 minutes or until the vegetables are tender.
3. Working in batches, transfer the mixture to a food processor or blender; purée until smooth (or purée in the pot with an immersion blender).
4. Return the soup to simmer; stir in the half and half. Season with salt and pepper; stir in the parsley. Simmer until heated through.
5. To serve, ladle the soup into bowls; garnish with the celery leaves or chives. Serve with brown bread.

STEAMED IRISH MUSSELS IN CIDER CREAM

Serves 2

JOHNNIE FOX'S Pub in Glencullen, County Dublin, is one of Ireland's oldest traditional pubs and renowned for being "the highest pub in the country." Dating from 1798, the pub is a treasure trove of memorabilia, and the restaurant/pub is renowned for its Hooley Night (an Irish dancing show with traditional music) and extensive seafood menu, including this dish of cider-steamed Irish mussels. Serve it with one of the brown breads on pages 27, 28, and 29.

- 1 1/4 cups dry cider, such as the Bulmers brand
- 1 1/2 cups dry white wine, divided
- 1 onion, chopped
- 2 bay leaves
- 4 tablespoons mixed fresh herbs
- 2 tablespoons minced garlic
- 1 teaspoon red pepper flakes
- 1 fish stock cube, such as the Knorr brand
- 5 cups heavy whipping cream
- Cornstarch, as need (to thicken)
- Salt
- Ground black pepper
- 2 1/4 pounds mussels, scrubbed and debearded
- 1 cup water
- Chopped fresh flat-leaf parsley, for garnish
- Lemon wedges, for garnish

1. In a large stockpot, bring the cider, 1 cup of the wine, onion, bay leaves, mixed herbs, garlic, and red pepper flakes to a boil. Reduce heat to simmer; cook for 10 to 15 minutes or until reduced by half.
2. Add the stock cube and cream; return to boil. Add the remaining 1/4 cup of wine. Thicken with a mixture of cornstarch whisked with water for a thicker sauce. Season with salt and pepper.
3. In a large stockpot, steam the mussels over medium heat in salted water for 6 to 10 minutes or until they open (discarding any that do not open). With a slotted spoon, add the mussels to the stock.
4. To serve, ladle the mussels into shallow bowls; garnish with parsley and lemon wedges. Serve with brown bread.

Andikdublin/Fáilte Ireland

ROOT VEGETABLE & RED LENTIL SOUP

Serves 4 to 6

AVOCA is one of the most recognizable names in Ireland. From a cooperative weaving mill founded in 1732 on the banks of the Avoca River in Wicklow, to a thriving handweaving business in the 1970s, to a collection of popular and well-loved food markets and cafés started in the 1980s, Avoca has led a revolution in Irish crafts and has become a champion of seasonal, locally sourced ingredients. This popular soup fuses the flavors of traditional root vegetables with the punch of chilli, ginger, and red lentils. Serve it with one of the brown breads on pages 27, 28, and 29.

- 2 tablespoons butter
- 1 large onion, chopped
- 2 celery stalks, chopped
- 3 carrots, chopped
- 1 parsnip, chopped
- 1 small sweet potato, cut into 1 1/2-inch pieces
- 1/2 butternut squash, cut into 1 1/2-inch pieces
- 1/2 small chilli, deseeded (optional)
- 1/2-inch piece fresh ginger, peeled and chopped
- 5 cups canned low-sodium vegetable broth, plus more if needed
- 1 spring fresh thyme, plus more for garnish
- 6 ounces orange lentils, rinsed
- 2 to 3 tablespoons heavy whipping cream, plus more for serving
- Salt
- Ground black pepper
- Chopped fresh flat-leaf parsley, for garnish

1. In a large saucepan, melt the butter over medium heat. Add the onions and celery. Cook for 3 to 5 minutes or until soft but browned.
2. Add the carrots, parsnip, sweet potato, squash, chilli (if using), and ginger. Cook, stirring occasionally, for 5 to 8 minutes or until the vegetables begin to soften.
3. Add the broth and thyme. Cook, covered, for about 30 minutes or until the vegetables are tender.
4. Add the lentils; cook for 8 to 10 minutes longer or until the lentils are cooked through. Remove from heat; let cool for 10 to 15 minutes.
5. Working in batches, transfer the soup to a food processor or blender; purée until smooth (or purée in the pot with an immersion blender). Return the soup to simmer; thin with additional stock, if needed. Stir in the cream. Season with salt and pepper. Simmer until heated through. To serve, ladle the soup into bowls; swirl in additional cream, if desired. Garnish with parsley. Serve with brown bread.

LAMB CROQUETTES

Makes 10 to 12

Tapas are traditional Spanish and Portuguese appetizers offered with a drink at bars and cafés. The popular "small bites" are now found internationally, including at pubs and wine bars throughout Ireland. These *croquetas*, made with lamb and mashed potatoes, are reminiscent of a Sunday roast meal, complete with the mint sauce for dipping. You can make the croquettes with leftovers if you have them, but you can also use ground lamb as in this recipe. (If using leftover lamb, chop and then pulse 4 to 5 times in a food processor.) For traditional Irish flavor, serve the croquettes with creamy mint sauce.

- 8 ounces ground lamb
- 1 cup mashed potatoes
- 2 tablespoons grated Parmesan cheese
- 3 tablespoons chopped fresh flat-leaf parsley
- 2 tablespoons chopped fresh mint
- 1 tablespoon lemon zest
- 1 teaspoon fresh rosemary
- Salt
- Ground black pepper
- Flour, for dredging
- 1 egg, beaten with 1 tablespoon water, for egg wash
- Panko breadcrumbs, for dredging
- Canola oil, for frying
- Fresh mint, for garnish

1. In a large bowl, combine the lamb, potatoes, cheese, parsley, mint, zest, rosemary, salt, and pepper; mix well. Divide the mixture into 10 to 12 evenly sized pieces; shape into small logs.
2. Roll each log into flour, shaking off excess. Dredge in egg wash; roll in breadcrumbs. Transfer to a large platter; refrigerate for 30 minutes to firm.
3. Preheat the oven to 350°F. Line a baking sheet with parchment paper.
4. In a large nonstick skillet, heat about 3 tablespoons of oil over medium heat.
5. Working in batches, fry the croquettes, turning frequently, for 6 to 8 minutes or until crisp and golden. Transfer to the prepared pan.
6. Bake the croquettes for 10 to 12 minutes or until the internal temperature reaches 160°F.
7. Let the croquettes rest for about 10 minutes before serving with the sauce.

CREAMY MINT SAUCE

Makes 1 1/2 cups

- 1 cup Greek yogurt
- 1/2 cup sour cream
- 3 to 4 tablespoons finely chopped fresh mint
- 2 teaspoons minced garlic
- 1 teaspoon salt
- 1/2 teaspoon ground black pepper
- 1 tablespoon fresh lemon juice

1. In a small bowl, whisk together all ingredients until smooth.
2. Refrigerate for 30 minutes before serving.
3. Cover and refrigerate for up to 3 days.

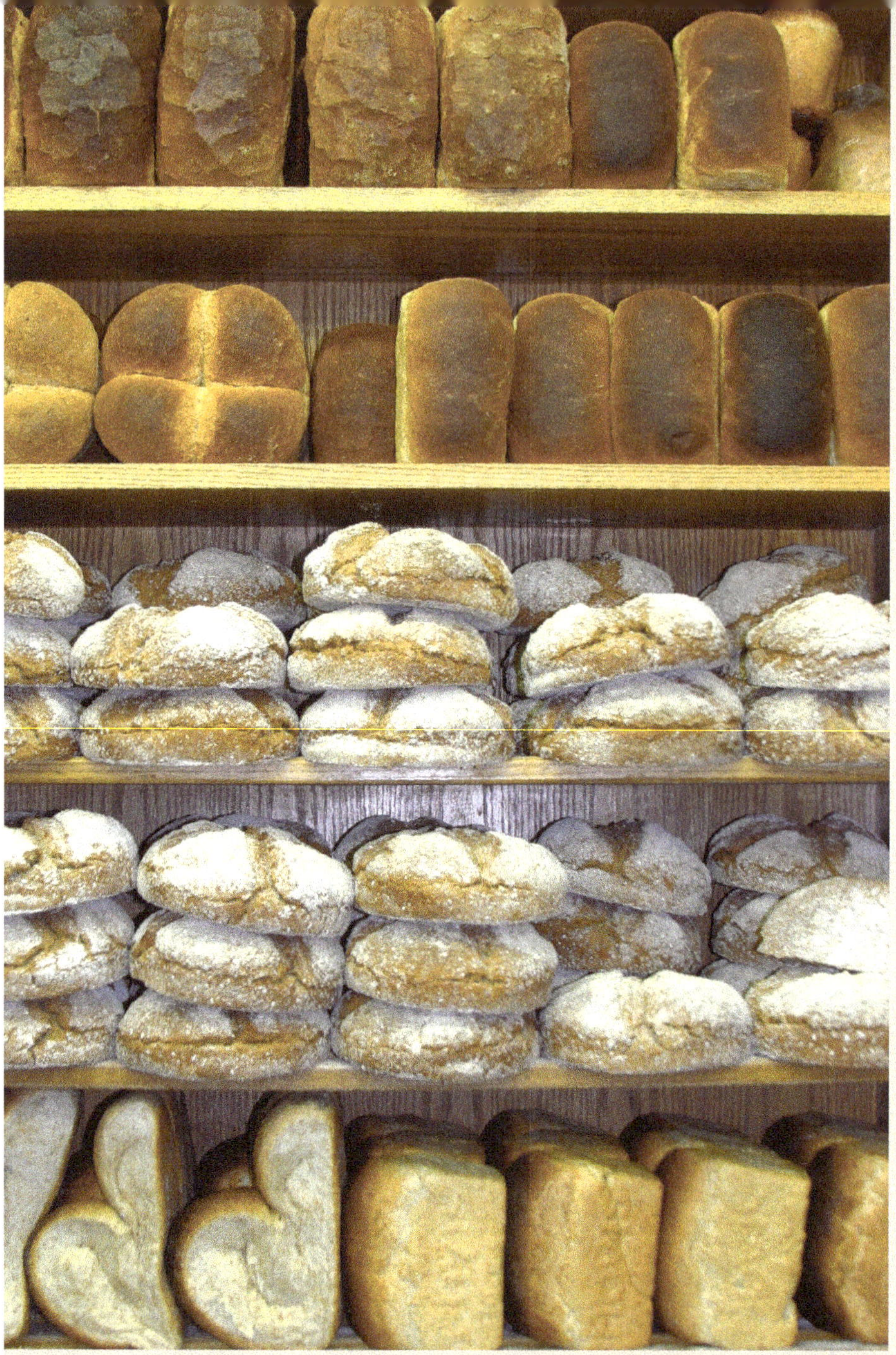

EST. 1887
BARRON'S
BAKERY &
COFFEE HOUSE

Belfast
Baps

Guinness
Wheaten

Est. 1876
GRIFFIN'S
BAKERY

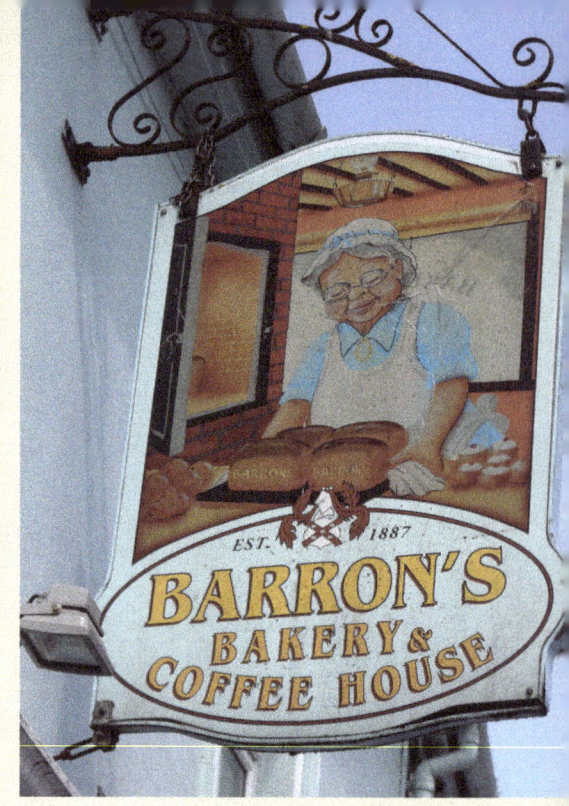

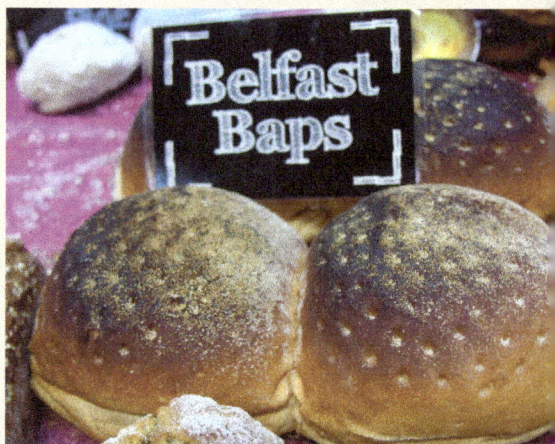

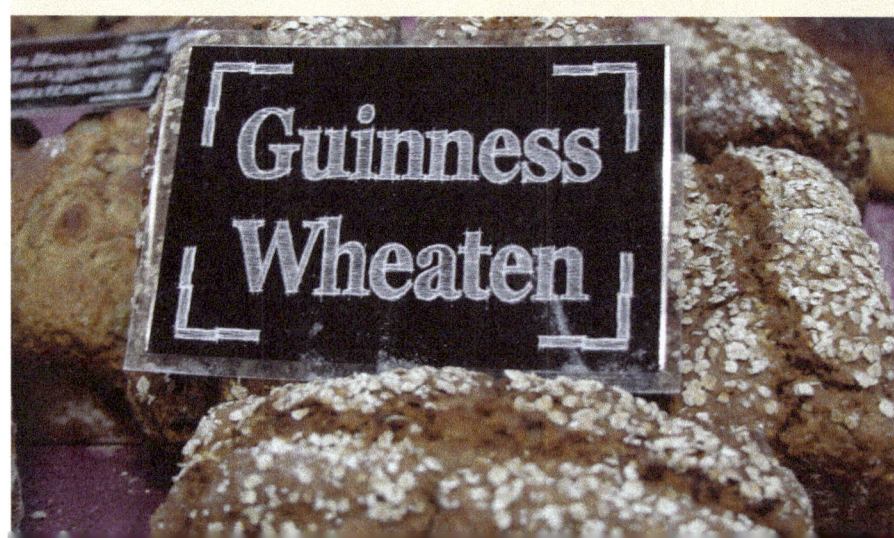

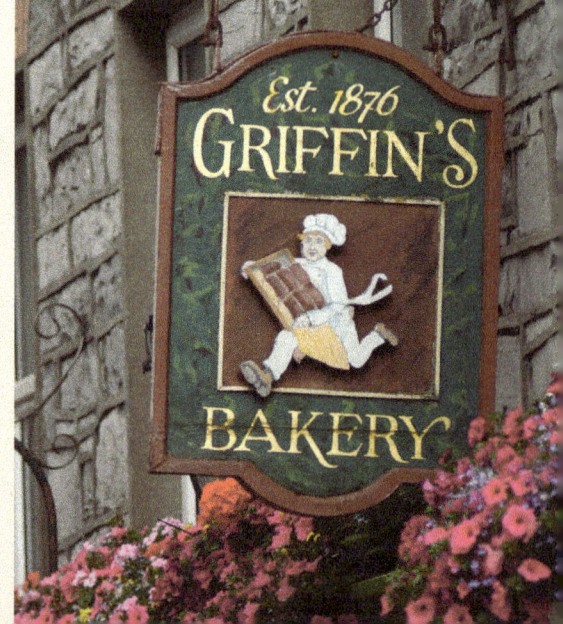

KINSALE BROWN SODA BREAD

Makes 1 loaf

Remember that brown bread is a good familiar creature and worth more than his weight in flesh.
—George Bernard Shaw, Irish playwright

George Bernard Shaw loved brown soda bread. Chances are he never imagined this homey loaf would evolve into iconic status with nearly as many variations as there are cooks. Throughout my travels in Ireland, I discovered it comes in all shapes and sizes and has many secret ingredients, such as this one from a bakery in Kinsale, County Cork, which gets its moist interior from Italian olive oil! For an herb-flavored bread, the chef suggested adding 1 to 2 tablespoons minced fresh herbs, 1 tablespoon fennel seeds, and 1 tablespoon poppy seeds.

- 2 cups coarse whole wheat flour[1]
- 1/2 teaspoon baking soda
- 1/8 teaspoon salt
- 2 tablespoons sugar
- 1/4 cup extra virgin olive oil
- 1/4 cup canola oil
- 1 cup buttermilk, plus more if needed
- 1 tablespoon sesame seeds
- Softened butter, for serving

1. Preheat the oven to 400°F. Coat an 8-inch loaf pan with no-stick baking spray with flour.
2. In a large bowl, whisk together the flour, baking soda, salt, and sugar.
3. In another bowl, whisk together the olive oil, canola oil, and buttermilk. Make a well in the center of the flour mixture; stir in the liquid until soft dough forms.
4. Transfer the mixture to the prepared pan. Smooth the top with a spatula dipped in buttermilk. Sprinkle with sesame seeds. Run a knife lengthwise down the center to help with rising.
5. Bake the bread for 30 minutes. Reduce the oven temperature to 350°F. Bake for 25 to 30 minutes longer or until a skewer inserted into the center comes out clean. Let cool on a wire rack for about 30 minutes before slicing. Serve slices spread with butter.

---

[1] King Arthur Baking Company makes Irish-Style wholemeal flour that works well in this recipe (kingarthurbaking.com).

Opposite page (clockwise, from top left): GRIFFIN'S BAKERY, Galway; BARRON'S BAKERY, Cappoquin, Co. Waterford; ST. GEORGE'S MARKET, Belfast; GRIFFIN'S BAKERY, Galway; ST. GEORGE'S MARKET, Belfast. *All photos Margaret M. Johnson*

GUINNESS & MALT WHEATEN BREAD

Makes 1 loaf

In true Irish fashion, this recipe comes with a story and *two* unusual ingredients—Guinness and barley malt syrup (a sweet, treacle-like syrup). Sometime in the 1990s, I enjoyed this bread at breakfast in a small hotel in Belfast. Toasted to perfection, it arrived with hand-churned butter and homemade preserves. I complimented the hostess and asked if she would share her recipe. She confessed it was made at a nearby bakery but would source the recipe for me. She did, and I've been making it ever since.

- 1 cup fine whole wheat flour, plus more for sprinkling
- 1 cup coarse whole wheat flour[1]
- 1/4 cup sugar
- 1/2 teaspoon baking soda
- 1/2 teaspoon salt
- 4 tablespoons unsalted butter, cut into small pieces
- 3/4 cup buttermilk
- 3/4 cup Guinness Stout
- 1 tablespoon barley malt extract[2]
- Softened butter, for spreading

1. Preheat the oven to 375°F. Coat an 8-inch loaf pan with no-stick baking spray. Sprinkle with whole wheat flour; tap out excess.
2. In a large bowl, whisk together the flours, sugar, baking soda, and salt. With a pastry cutter, your fingers, or two forks, work or cut in the butter until the mixture resembles coarse crumbs.
3. Make a well in the center. Add the buttermilk, Guinness, and malt; mix with a wooden spoon (dough will have a porridge consistency). Transfer the mixture to the prepared pan; sprinkle additional flour on top.
4. Bake the bread for 30 minutes. Reduce the oven temperature to 325°F. Bake for 30 minutes longer or until a skewer inserted into the center comes out clean.
5. Turn off the oven. Let the bread cool with the door open for 30 minutes.
6. Let cool completely on a wire rack for about 30 minutes before slicing. Serve slices spread with butter.

---

[1] King Arthur Baking Company makes Irish-style wholemeal flour that works well in this recipe (kingarthurbaking.com)

[2] Barley malt extract is available in health food stores. Eden Foods is one brand I recommend.

WALNUT & TREACLE BREAD

Makes 1 loaf

At Ballynahinch Castle in Recess, Connemara, both dark treacle (a by-product of the sugar-refining process) and Greek yogurt are added to the nutty brown bread served in both its fine dining Owenmore Restaurant and the casual Fisherman's Pub and Ranji Room. Treacle is made in a two varieties—light, known as golden syrup; and dark, which is more like what Americans call molasses. The darker variety, used in this recipe, imparts a distinctive caramel-like flavor. The Lyle's brand is one of the most well-known in Ireland and the United Kingdom and can be found in some supermarkets and online from a number of sites.

- 2 1/2 cups whole wheat flour[1]
- 1 cup all-purpose flour
- 1/4 cup (packed) dark brown sugar
- 1/4 cup Irish oatmeal, such as the Flahavan's or McCann's brand
- 1 1/2 teaspoons baking soda
- 1 1/2 teaspoons baking powder
- 1/4 teaspoon salt
- 1/2 cup plain Greek yogurt
- 5 tablespoons unsalted butter, melted and cooled
- 1 1/2 cups buttermilk
- 1 large egg
- 1/3 cup dark treacle
- 1/4 cup chopped walnuts
- Softened butter, for spreading

1. Preheat the oven to 300°F. Coat an 8-inch loaf pan with no-stick baking spray with flour.
2. In a large bowl, whisk together the flours, sugar, oatmeal, baking soda, baking powder, and salt.
3. In another bowl, whisk together the yogurt, butter, buttermilk, egg, and treacle. Make a well in the center of the flour mixture.
4. Add the buttermilk mixture; stir to blend. Fold in the walnuts. Transfer the mixture to the prepared pan.
5. Bake the bread for 45 to 50 minutes or until a skewer inserted into the center comes out clean. Turn the bread out of the pan.
6. Return to the oven; bake directly on the rack for a further 10 minutes.
7. Let cool completely on a wire rack before slicing. Serve slices spread with butter.

---

1   King Arthur Baking Company makes Irish-style wholemeal flour that works well in this recipe (kingarthurbaking.com)

CASHEL BLUE TARTINE WITH ROASTED FIGS & PROSCIUTTO

Serves 4

Cashel Blue, Ireland's first farmhouse blue cheese, is recognized for its creamy texture, buttery color, and distinctive flavor. It's imported to the U.S. by Kerrygold, making it widely available in cheese shops and supermarkets to use in a salad, tart, cheese board, or this tartine—a chic, open-faced sandwich. To complement one of Ireland's best blue cheeses, use good sourdough bread, thyme-flavored figs, and the best prosciutto you can find. The trendy, French-inspired tartine is delicious served with a small salad tossed with walnut vinaigrette (see following recipe). For a vegetarian option, omit the prosciutto.

For the Figs:

- 4 fresh figs, cut into quarters
- 1 tablespoon brown sugar
- 1 tablespoon fresh thyme

For the Tartine:

- 3 tablespoons extra virgin olive oil
- Four 1/2-inch-thick slices sourdough bread
- 6 ounces Cashel Blue® cheese
- 4 slices prosciutto, cut in half
- 1 1/2 tablespoons honey
- Fresh thyme sprigs, for garnish
- Watercress or arugula (1/2 cup per person), for garnish

1. Preheat the oven to 350°F. Line a baking dish with parchment paper. Place the figs in the prepared pan; sprinkle with brown sugar and thyme. Roast for 10 to 12 minutes or until lightly browned.

2. Heat a grill pan over medium-high heat. Brush both sides of the bread with the olive oil. Grill for about 2 minutes on each side or until toasted. Remove to four serving plates. Roughly spread the Cashel Blue on one side of each toast.

3. To serve, arrange four fig quarters on top of the cheese; tuck in the slices of prosciutto. Drizzle with honey; garnish with thyme. Toss the watercress or arugula with the vinaigrette; serve alongside each tartine, if desired.

Margaret M. Johnson

WALNUT VINAIGRETTE

Makes 3/4 cup

- 1/2 cup walnut oil
- 2 tablespoons white wine vinegar
- 1 1/2 teaspoons Dijon mustard
- Salt
- Pepper

1. In a lidded jar, combine all ingredients.
2. Shake to blend.

BUFFALO CHEESE FROM CORK

In 2009, Cork farmer Johnny Lynch bought 30 buffaloes in Italy, brought them to Cork, and set up the first milking herd of buffaloes in Ireland. He now has more than 700 animals happily grazing on his farm based in Kilnamartyra, near Macroom, supplying the milk for his cheeses that include buffalo ricotta, mozzarella, burrata, bocconcini, halloumi (a Cypriot-style grilling cheese), and a Greek-style feta.

In 2011, Jenny-Rose Clarke and Toby Simmonds established Toons Bridge Dairy, sister company to The Real Olive Company, after discovering there was a real appetite for fresh mozzarella among their customers. In an old creamery building in the artisan-rich region of West Cork, they also began producing fresh buffalo mozzarella, and eventually other cheeses in the Mediterranean tradition. Working in small batches with fresh, local, and unpasteurized buffalo, cow, and sheep's milk, Toons Bridge Dairy specializes in Southern Mediterranean style cheeses such as mozzarella, caciocavallo, ricotta, smoked scamorza, halloumi, and burrata.

Monkey Business Images/Dreamstime

WILD MUSHROOM & RICOTTA TOAST

Serves 6

SOUNDING more like a starter you'd find on the menu of an Italian restaurant, these toasts feature 100 percent "made-in-Ireland" ingredients. Shiitake, oyster, maitake, and nameko are just a few of the wild mushroom varieties the Gorman family grows on wooden blocks at their Garryhinch Wood Exotic Mushroom Farm in County Offaly. Sautéed in butter and olive oil, the mushrooms top crisp brioche and creamy ricotta cheese made from the milk of Cork-reared buffaloes!

- 2 tablespoons butter
- 2 tablespoons extra virgin olive oil
- 16 ounces mixed wild mushrooms (such as shiitake, oyster, and enoki), divided
- 1 tablespoon finely chopped shallot
- 1 garlic clove, minced
- 1/4 cup dry white wine
- 2 tablespoons lemon juice
- 1 teaspoon finely chopped fresh thyme
- 1 tablespoon chopped fresh flat-leaf parsley
- Sea salt
- Ground black pepper
- Six 1/2-inch-thick brioche slices, cut in half
- 1 cup buffalo ricotta cheese
- 2 tablespoon chopped chives, for garnish

1. In a large skillet, melt 1 tablespoon of butter with 1 tablespoon of olive oil over medium heat. Add half the mushrooms. Cook, stirring frequently, for about 3 minutes or until the mushrooms are browned. With a slotted spoon, transfer the mushrooms to a bowl. Repeat with the remaining butter, oil, and mushrooms.

2. Stir in the shallots and garlic; cook for 2 to 3 minutes. Stir in the wine, lemon juice, thyme, and parsley; cook for 2 minutes. With a slotted spoon, transfer the mixture to the bowl with the other mushrooms. Season with salt and pepper.

3. Preheat the oven to 350°F. Place the brioche slices in a single layer on a wire rack on a baking sheet. Bake for about 5 minutes on each side or until toasted and lightly browned. Remove from oven.

4. Spread the cheese evenly over each toast. Divide the mushroom mixture evenly over the toast; sprinkle with chives.

GOAT CHEESE TARTS WITH RED ONION MARMALADE

Makes 12

LOYALTY to local products is one of the hallmarks of Irish cooking. Chefs and home cooks alike share this ethos, especially when it comes to dairy products like cheese, which is most often named for the farm where it's made, often just down the road—St. Tola in Clare or Ardsallagh in Cork are two good examples. If you have a local goat cheese, do the same. The red onion marmalade is also a delicious accompaniment to brie and cheddar.

RED ONION MARMALADE
Makes 1 1/2 cups

- 2 tablespoons extra virgin olive oil
- 3 medium red onions, peeled, halved, and cut into thin slices
- 1/2 cup packed dark brown sugar
- 2 tablespoons red wine vinegar
- 1 tablespoon fresh thyme leaves
- Salt
- Ground black pepper

1. In a medium saucepan, heat the oil over medium heat.
2. Add the onions. Cook, stirring once or twice, for about 10 minutes or until wilted.
3. Stir in the sugar and vinegar.
4. Cook for 30 to 35 minutes longer or until the mixture thickens.
5. Stir in the thyme, salt, and pepper.
6. Remove from heat. Let cool.

For the Tarts:

- 1 sheet frozen puff pastry, such as the Pepperidge Farm brand, thawed
- Twelve 1/2-inch-thick slices goat cheese
- 8 ounces goat cheese, crumbled
- 1 egg beaten with 1 tablespoon water, for egg wash
- Thyme sprigs, for garnish
- Pine nuts, for sprinkling (optional)

Ingrid Balabanova/Dreamstime

1. Preheat the oven to 400°F. Line 2 baking pans with parchment paper.

2. Unfold the pastry sheet on a floured surface. Cut the sheet into 3 strips along the fold lines; cut each strip into 4 pieces.

3. With the tip of a sharp knife, score a 1/2-inch-wide border from the edge of each square (do not cut all the way thorough). Make another 1/2-inch cut in each corner, cutting all the way through. Transfer 6 pastry pieces to each prepared pan, spacing 1/2 inch apart.

4. Spread 1/2 tablespoon of the onion marmalade inside the center of the pastry (cover and refrigerate the rest for another use). Top with the crumbled cheese.

5. Brush the pastry border with the egg wash.

6. Bake the tarts for 15 to 20 minutes or until puffed and golden.

7. To serve, garnish each tart with a sprig of thyme. Sprinkle with pine nuts, if desired. (To make ahead, store the cooled tarts in a single layer in an airtight container; refrigerate for up to 2 days. Reheat in a preheated 350°F oven for 5 to 7 minutes or until heated through).

GOAT CHEESE & TOMATO CHARLOTTES

Serves 6

SLOW-ROASTING tomatoes gives them a rich flavor that adds depth to sauces, tarts, and this soufflé-like dish made with goat cheese. The dish is an invention of Denis Cotter, chef-proprietor of Paradiso, the vegetarian restaurant he established in Cork in 1993. In his *Café Paradiso Cookbook*, he said, "Every season has at least one hero and it is these vegetables that structure our year and dominate our menus during their high season."[1]

In summer, tomatoes are one of the heroes, served originally in these small soufflés over a bed of puy lentils with wedges of polenta; but they are equally delicious sitting on a bed of steamed spinach or next to a salad of mixed greens dressed with your favorite vinaigrette. Thirty years on, Cotter still serves some of the most imaginative vegetarian food in Ireland, ranging from smoky za'atar roast squash to grilled dan dan cauliflower and napa cabbage curry, three recipes featured in his latest book *Paradiso*.[2] (For more on the popularity of vegetarian and vegan options in Ireland today, see page 70)

For the Tomatoes:

- 6 large beefsteak tomatoes
- Sea salt
- Ground black pepper
- Extra virgin olive oil

For the Filling:

- 3 garlic cloves
- 16 ounces goat cheese, at room temperature
- 8 ounces cream cheese, at room temperature
- 2 large eggs
- 3 large egg whites
- 1/3 to 1/2 cup half and half
- 4 to 5 fresh basil leaves, chopped
- Ground black pepper
- Steamed spinach, for serving (optional

---

1 Denis Cotter, *Café Paradiso Cookbook* (Cork: Atrium Press, 1999).
2 Denis Cotter, *Paradiso* (Dublin: Nine Beans Rows Books, 2023).

1. Preheat the oven to 350°F. Lightly brush two baking sheets with olive oil. Cut each tomato horizontally into 3 thick slices; place on the prepared pans. Season with salt and pepper; brush with olive oil.

2. Roast, turning once, for 60 to 75 minutes or until partly dried and slightly caramelized. Set aside.

3. Increase the oven temperature to 375°F.

4. Butter six 8-ounce ramekins. Line the bottom of each ramekin with a round of parchment paper.

5. In a food processor, combine the garlic, goat cheese, cream cheese, and eggs; process for 1 to 2 minutes or until smooth.

6. With the machine running, add the egg whites, one at a time; process for 30 seconds or until blended.

7. Transfer the mixture to a medium bowl and stir in enough half and half to give a thick, pouring consistency.

8. Stir in the basil and pepper.

9. Put a tomato slice in the bottom of each ramekin; top with a tablespoon of cheese mixture. Repeat twice to make 3 layers in each ramekin.

10. Place the dishes in a roasting pan filled with enough hot water to come halfway up the sides.

11. Bake for 35 to 40 minutes or until the filling is set in the center.

12. Remove the pan from the oven; let dishes sit in the pan for 5 minutes.

13. To serve, run a sharp knife around the sides of the dishes to loosen. Invert onto the center of each of six salad plates; remove the parchment. (If serving with steamed spinach, put some of the spinach in the center of the plates; invert the dishes onto the spinach).

Nicoleta Raftu/Dreamstime

ROASTED BEETROOT & CITRUS SALAD WITH CASHEL BLUE CHEESE

Serves 6

CASHEL Blue is celebrating forty years of crafting Ireland's most well-known blue cheese at their farm near Fethard in County Tipperary. When you pair the salty blue with earthy beets (called "beetroot" in Ireland and the United Kingdom) and tart citrus, it's a match made in heaven. With beets ranging in color from white to golden to purple and red, this salad is as pretty as it is delicious. Roast the beets in separate packets to prevent the colors from bleeding up to a day ahead, but save the remaining ones for another dish. Blend the dressing and use a mix of your favorite lettuce and arugula for a perfect starter. Serve it with citrus dressing (recipe follows).

- Mixed greens with arugula (1 1/2 to 2 cups per person)
- 2 roasted golden beets, sliced
- 2 roasted red beets, sliced
- 1 medium seedless orange, peeled and sliced
- 1 tangerine or mandarin orange, peeled and segmented
- 4 ounces crumbled Cashel Blue Cheese[1]
- Citrus dressing

1. Divide the mixed greens among six salad plates. Arrange the beets and oranges on top; sprinkle with the cheese.
2. Spoon the dressing over the salad just before serving.

Roasted Beetroot:

- 4 golden beets
- 4 red beets
- 1 tablespoon extra virgin olive oil

---

[1] Cashel Blue is distributed in the U.S. by Kerrygold and is widely available in cheese shops and major supermarkets such as Whole Foods, Trader Joe's, Publix, and Safeway.

Vanillaechoes/Dreamstime

Roasted Beetroot (cont.)

1. Preheat the oven to 450°F.
2. Cut off the green tops and root ends of the beets. Toss the beetroots with extra virgin olive oil; wrap in a foil packet.
3. Place the packets on a baking sheet; roast for 60 to 75 minutes or until the beets are easily pierced with the tip of a knife. (Roasting times will vary depending on the size of the beets, so use those of similar size).
4. Remove from the oven; set aside until cool enough to handle. Remove the beets from packets. To prevent hands from staining, wear gloves or rub the skins off under cold running water.
5. Cover and refrigerate for up to three days.

CITRUS DRESSING

Makes 1 cup

- 1/3 cup fresh orange juice
- 3 teaspoons orange zest
- 1 1/2 tablespoons honey
- 1/3 cup canola oil
- 1/2 teaspoon Dijon mustard
- 1/4 teaspoon salt
- 1/4 teaspoon ground black pepper
- 2 teaspoons poppy seeds

1. In a lidded jar, combine everything but the poppy seeds.
2. Cover; shake until blended.
3. Stir in poppy seeds.
4. Refrigerate until serving time.

WARM MUSHROOM & BLACK PUDDING SALAD

Serves 4

BLACK and white puddings have been the mainstay of an Irish breakfast for generations, served alongside eggs, bacon (rashers), sausages (bangers), grilled tomatoes, and mushrooms. In the 1880s, Philip Harrington developed the secret spice mix recipe for the puddings he made at his butcher shop in Clonakilty, County Cork. The Clonakilty brand remains one of Ireland's most popular. The business, including the shop and the recipe, was eventually sold to the Twomey family in 1976; and now Colette Twomey is the sole keeper of the spice mix that's guarded with near-religious secrecy.

Today, there are several black pudding brands in Ireland (including housemade at local butcher shops); and the spicy beef blood, beef meat, and oatmeal sausage is served in dishes well beyond the morning fry-up (white pudding, also popular as a breakfast dish, uses pork in place of beef). You'll find it topping a crostini with apples, blended with potatoes in a croquette, and tossed with bacon and warm wild mushrooms (see Garryhinch Exotic Wood Mushrooms on page 33) in this earthy salad. Serve it with wholegrain mustard vinaigrette (recipe follows).

- 2 tablespoons extra virgin olive oil
- 4 slices Irish bacon
- 12 slices black pudding[1]
- 4 tablespoons butter
- 1 tablespoon chopped fresh chives
- 1 tablespoon minced shallot
- 8 ounces mixed wild mushrooms
- 1 teaspoon fresh lemon juice
- Salt
- Ground black pepper
- Mixed greens (1 1/2 to 2 cups per person)

---

[1] In the U.S., you can substitute Tommy Moloney's brand of black pudding (tommymoloneys.com).

Margaret M. Johnson

1. In a large skillet over medium heat, heat the olive oil. Fry the bacon on each side for 3 to 5 minutes or until browned. Roughly chop.
2. Fry the black pudding for 3 to 5 minutes or until cooked through.
3. Wipe out the pan; return to medium heat. Melt the butter.
4. Add the chives, shallot, and mushrooms; sauté for 3 to 4 minutes or until soft but not browned.
5. Stir in the lemon juice, salt, and pepper.
6. To serve, divide the mixed greens among four salad plates; toss with bacon and 2 to 3 tablespoons of the vinaigrette (cover and refrigerate remaining vinaigrette for another salad). Place three slices of pudding on each salad; spoon the warm mushrooms and juices on top.

WHOLEGRAIN MUSTARD VINAIGRETTE

Makes about 1 cup

- 1 tablespoon wholegrain mustard
- 1 tablespoon Dijon mustard
- 1 teaspoon honey
- 2 tablespoons white wine vinegar or white balsamic vinegar
- 1/2 cup extra virgin olive oil
- 1/2 teaspoon fresh lemon juice
- 1/4 teaspoon salt
- 1/4 teaspoon ground black pepper

1. In a lidded jar, combine all ingredients.
2. Shake to blend.
3. Refrigerate until serving time.

Natalia Zhekova/Dreamstime

HOT SMOKED SALMON CHOWDER

Serves 6

THE Burren Smokehouse in Lisdoonvarna, County Clare, is a perennial winner in food competitions such as *Blas na hÉireann*, which honors the best Irish producers, and The Great Taste Awards, administered by the U.K. Guild of Fine Food. The smokehouse, founded in 1989 by the Curtin family, smokes organic Irish salmon using both hot and cold smoking methods, flavoring some with spices; some with honey, whiskey and fennel; and some with honey, lemon, and pepper that's used in this recipe for salmon chowder. (Alternately, use plain smoked salmon and add a pinch of lemon and pepper seasoning.) Serve it with one of the brown breads on pages 27, 28, and 29.

- 1 tablespoon extra virgin olive oil
- 3 medium leeks (white and light green parts only), rinsed and sliced
- 1 tablespoon minced garlic
- 1 large russet potato, peeled and cut into 1-inch pieces
- 1 celery stalk, chopped
- 1/2 teaspoon salt
- 1/2 teaspoon ground black pepper
- 2 cups canned low-sodium vegetable broth
- 2 tablespoons tomato purée
- 2 cups milk
- 13 ounces Burren Smokehouse Hot Smoked Salmon with Honey, Lemon, and Pepper, flaked
- 1/2 cup heavy whipping cream
- 2 tablespoons chopped fresh chives, for garnish

1. In a large saucepan, heat the olive oil over medium heat. Add the leeks; cook for 2 minutes or until soft but not browned. Add the garlic, potato, celery, salt, and pepper; stir to coat.
2. Add the broth; simmer for about 15 minutes or until the potatoes are tender.
3. Stir in the tomato purée and milk. Return the soup to simmer, making sure to not boil.
4. Stir in the salmon. When heated through, gently stir in the cream.
5. To serve, ladle the chowder into shallow bowls; garnish with chives. Serve with brown bread.

CHILLI-SMOKED SALMON FRITTERS

Makes about 25

Frank Hederman's smoked products, perfected over the course of forty years at his smokehouse in Belvelly, near Cobh in County Cork, are among Ireland's most coveted foods. In 2022, he was the first Irish person honored with the prestigious *Walter Scheel Medaille*, an award that recognizes services to the preservation of European culinary traditions. Inspired by a tapas-like snack he found in Portugal, a friend of Hederman's created this recipe using hot smoked salmon with chillis for a delicious fritter that strikes a simultaneous sweet, savory, tangy flavor. (Alternately, use plain smoked salmon and add a pinch of chilli flakes). Serve the fritters with sweet chilli lime sauce and celeriac apple remoulade (recipes follow), a dish similar to coleslaw that substitutes julienne celeriac (celery root) for shredded cabbage, if desired.

- 2 1/2 cups mashed potatoes
- 1 small onion, chopped
- 2 tablespoons chopped fresh flat-leaf parsley
- 10 ounces Hederman's Hot Smoked Salmon with Chillis, flaked
- 1 teaspoon sea salt
- 1/2 teaspoon ground black pepper
- 1 large egg, beaten
- 1 tablespoon flour
- Sunflower oil, for frying
- Mixed greens, for garnish

1. In a large bowl, combine potatoes, onion, parsley, salmon, salt, and pepper; mix well. Stir in egg and flour; mix again.
2. Divide the mixture into about 25 evenly sized pieces; shape into small ovals or rounds.
3. Transfer fritters to a parchment-lined baking sheet; refrigerate for about 2 hours, or until chilled.
4. In a deep saucepan or fryer, heat the oil to 350°F. Working in batches, drop 5 to 6 fritters at a time into the oil; fry for about 1 minute, or until crisp and golden. With a slotted spoon, transfer to a wire rack set over a baking sheet (do not use a paper towel as this creates soggy rather than crisp fritters). Return the oil temperature to 350°F for each batch.
5. To serve, arrange fritters on a platter; serve with sauce and celeriac remoulade, if desired. Garnish with mixed greens.

SWEET CHILLI LIME SAUCE

Make about 1 cup

- 1 cup Greek yogurt
- 1 tablespoon sweet chilli sauce
- 2 teaspoons fresh lime juice
- 1/4 teaspoon salt
- 1/4 teaspoon pepper

1. In a small bowl, whisk together all ingredients.

CELERIAC & APPLE REMOULADE

Serves 4

- 1 medium celeriac
- 1 medium apple
- Lemon juice (to prevent browning)
- 1/3 cup mayonnaise
- 2 tablespoons Dijon mustard
- 1/2 teaspoon sugar
- 1 teaspoon salt
- 1/2 teaspoon black pepper
- 1 tablespoon fresh flat-leaf parsley

1. Peel and cut the celeriac into 1/8-inch-thick matchstick pieces.
2. Peel, core, and cut the apple into 1/8-inch-thick matchstick pieces. As you cut, add it to a bowl and sprinkle with lemon juice to prevent browning.
3. In a large bowl, whisk together lemon juice, mayonnaise, Dijon mustard, sugar, salt, ground black pepper, and chopped fresh flat-leaf parsley.
4. Add the celeriac and apples; toss to combine.
5. Cover with plastic wrap; refrigerate for at least 2 hours. Refrigerate for up to 2 days.

Sláinte an bradáin chugat.

(May you be as healthy as the salmon.)
—Old Irish Saying

Legend has it that more than two thousand years ago, druids left oak-smoked salmon as an offering to the great Dagda, god of the pagan Irish. In the fifth century, oak-smoked salmon was to have been served at a feast in the banqueting hall at Tara, the seat of the high kings of Ireland. The ancient Irish hero Finn MacCool reportedly gained the gift of knowledge simply from cooking and tasting a salmon.

Folklore aside, smoking salmon has always had a practical side as well, namely as one of the primary ways to preserve food as a winter provision. Fortunately, the practice is very much alive and well today in smokehouses throughout Ireland, continuing the tradition that keeps smoked salmon one of the country's most treasured foods.

Frank Hederman smokes organically farmed salmon in Belvelly, County Cork, in one of only a handful of authentic, traditional timber smokehouses in Ireland. He sources his salmon from the waters near Clare Island off the west coast of Ireland; from May to mid-August, he buys fish caught by local fishermen in the estuary of Cork's River Lee. Hederman uses a pure, dry-salt cure and hangs his fish in small batches on tenterhooks over a beechwood fire. He also smokes mussels, eel, mackerel, butter, spices, nuts, seeds, and sundried tomatoes. His products are available at the smokehouse, at his stall in the English Market in Cork City, and online. To arrange a smokehouse tour, visit *www.frankhederman.com*.

The Burren Smokehouse in Lisdoonvarna, County Clare, is a smokehouse, visitor center, and gourmet food shop operated by the Curtin family. Founded in 1989, they produce organic oak-smoked salmon, trout, and mackerel in a facility that includes, in addition to the smokehouse, an exhibition kiln; smoke box; audio-visual presentation; and most recently, "Taste the Atlantic—The Salmon Experience," an interactive visitor space, where the story of salmon is told from its place in mythology to its role in modern aquaculture. To book a tour or order online, visit *www.burrensmokehouse.ie*.

Opposite page (clockwise, from top left): SMOKED SALMON WITH BROWN BREAD, Kivona/Dreamstime; HOT SMOKING MACKEREL AT FRANK HEDERMAN, Cobh, Co. Cork, Margaret M. Johnson; TASTE THE ATLANTIC - THE SALMON EXPERIENCE, Lisdoonvarna, Co. Clare, Margaret M. Johnson; HOT SMOKING SALMON, Alexander Groffen/Dreamstime; SEAWEED SMOKED SALMON, Margaret M. Johnson

Margaret M. Johnson

Anthony Creswell smokes organically farmed salmon at his smokehouse in Timoleague, County Cork. His father first started smoking the salmon he and his friends were catching on local rivers; later, in May 1988, Cresswell joined the business his father created. In addition to smoked salmon organically sourced from the waters off the west coast of Ireland, Ummera smoked products include gravadlax, smoked chicken, smoked duck, and smoked dry cured bacon. To order online, visit *www.ummera.com*.

Declan Droney and his wife Aoife founded Kinvara Smoked Salmon nearly twenty-five years ago in his native County Galway. Initially, they focused on wild salmon, but their concern about its sustainability led them to switch to smoking organic salmon, primarily from the waters near Clare Island. They continue to focus only on cold-smoking salmon, which is available online at *www.kinvarasmokedsalmon.com*.

Connemara Smokehouse in Ballyconnelley, County Galway, is one of Ireland's oldest traditional smokehouses. Located on the edge of Connemara, perched atop Bunowen Pier, it's been owned and operated by the Roberts family for three generations. They use traditional smoking methods for their products, which include organic salmon, gravadlax, mackerel, and tuna. To arrange a visit or to shop online, visit *www.smokehouse.ie*.

Sally Barnes smokes "only and always wild fish" at her Woodcock Smokery in Castletownshend, County Cork. She started traditional smoke-curing in 1979 as a way to preserve the fish she caught in the waters off the coast of West Cork. She continues that tradition using only sustainable quantities of fish from local boats taken during the very brief wild salmon season. A life-long preservationist and stalwart of small-scale independent business, Barnes offers master classes on salmon-smoking, leads coastal produce and mushroom foraging, and hosts a tasting menu of her smoked products for guests to enjoy in The Keep, the space at her smokery where she shares the near-lost art of preserving wild food. For details on her products or events, visit *www.woodcocksmokery.com*.

Fingal Ferguson's Gubbeen Smokehouse is an extension of his family's farming endeavor, one that began in the 1970s when his parents Tom and Giana started making cheese at their farm in Schull, County Cork. Fingal smokes a range of artisan pork products from pigs reared in straw pens (or entirely outdoors), producing dry cured bacon, salami, pepperoni, and chorizo, along with brined meats. To find his products online, visit *www.gubbeenfarmhouseproducts.com*.

Est.d 1324
BARS
LIVE MUSIC
KYTELERS
INN
HOT FOOD
SERVED ALL DAY

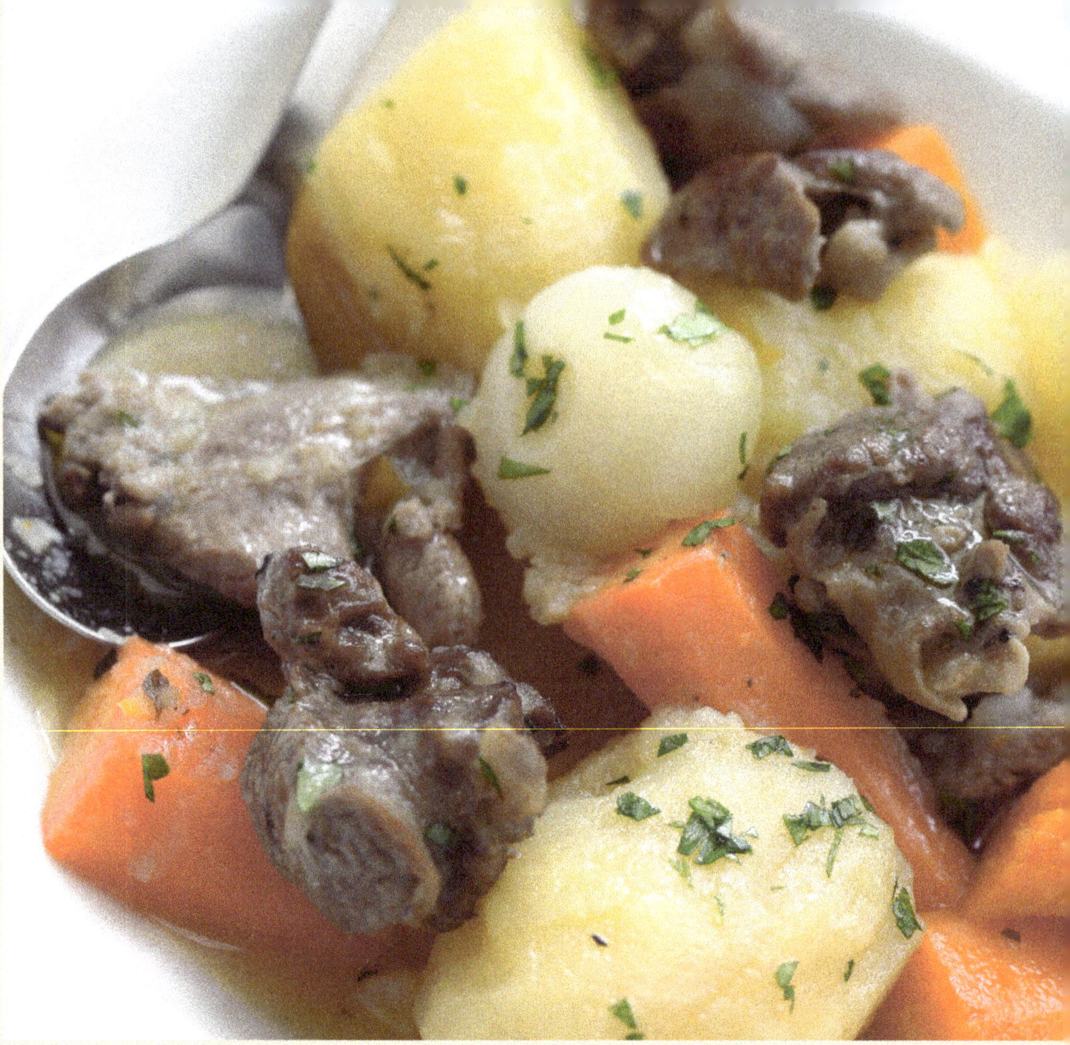

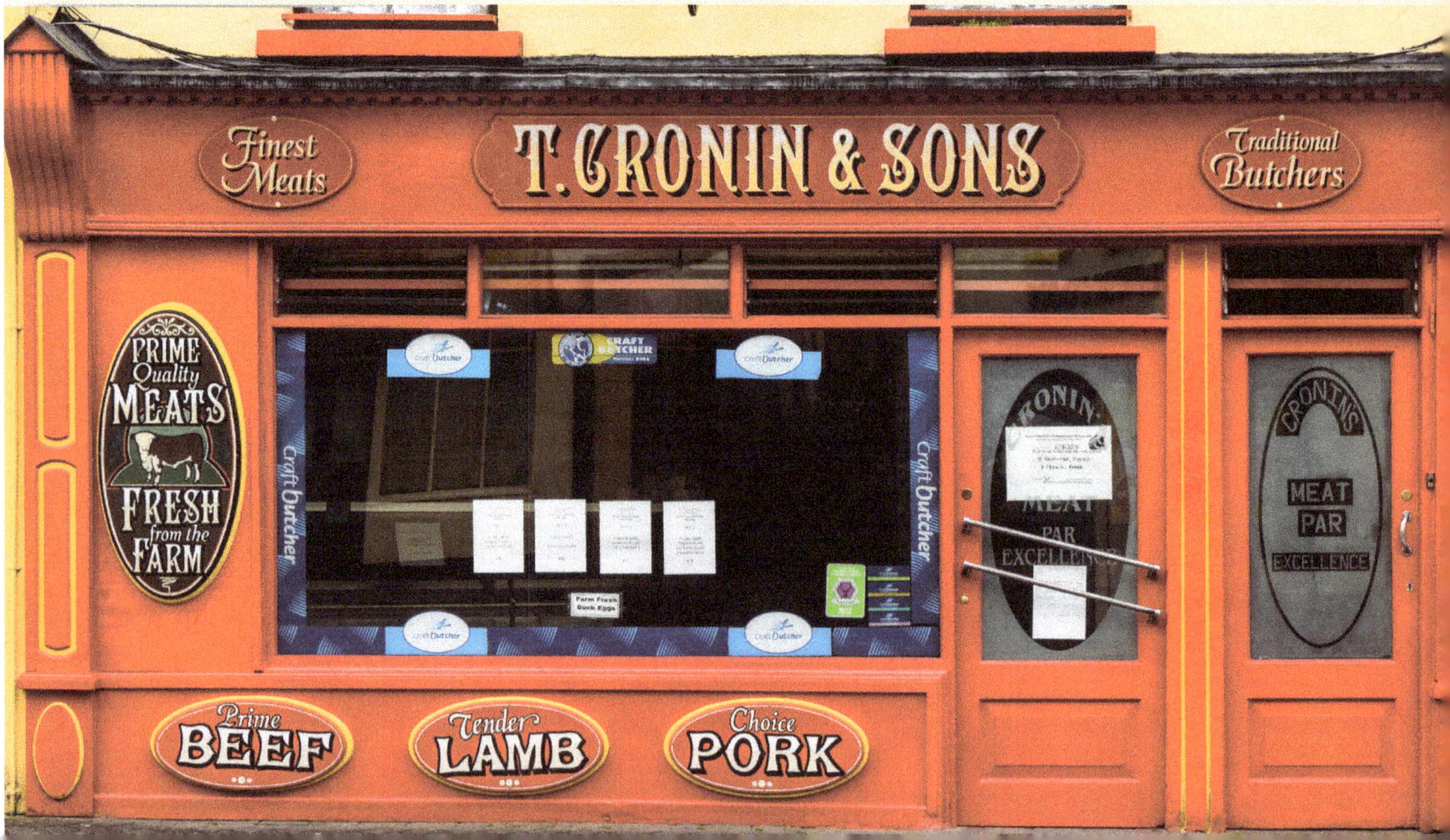
Finest Meats
T. CRONIN & SONS
Traditional Butchers
PRIME Quality MEATS
FRESH from the FARM
Craft Butcher
CRONINS
MEAT PAR EXCELLENCE
Prime BEEF
Tender LAMB
Choice PORK

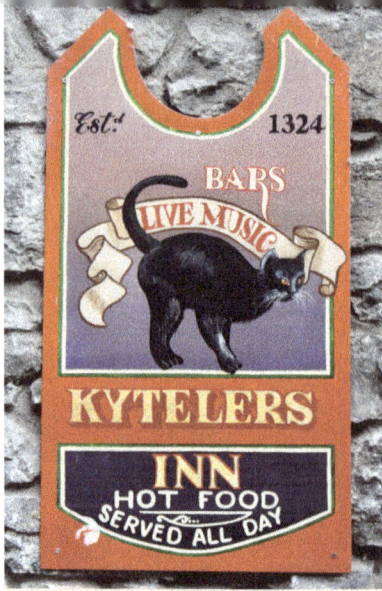

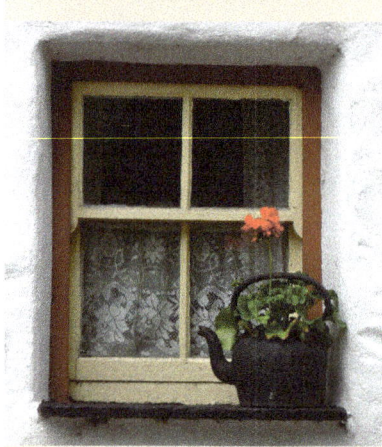

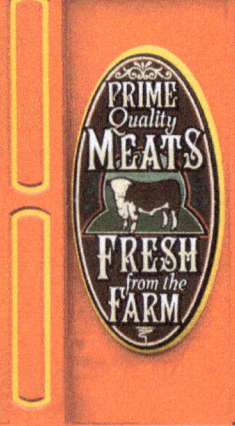

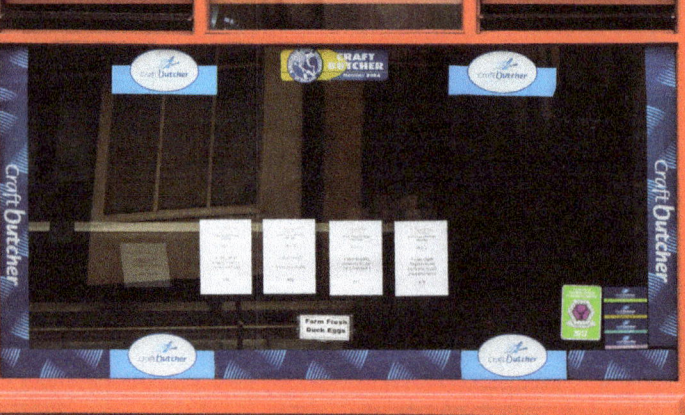

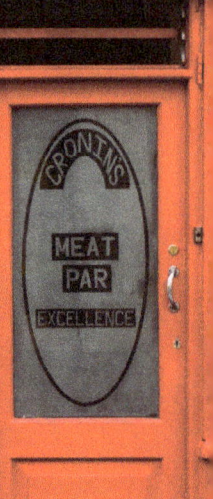

CHAPTER 2

MAINS
Meat, Fish, Poultry, & Vegetarian Entrées

*We can feel the beauty of a magnificent landscape perhaps,
but we can describe a leg of mutton and turnips better.*
—William Makepeace Thackeray, *The Irish Sketch Book*

Loin of Lamb with Parsley & Mint Sauce	52
Chimichurri	53
Lamb Chops with Honey, Apricot & Tarragon Sauce	54
Irish Stew	55
Shepherd's Pie With Cheddar Crust	56
Filet of Beef with Irish Whiskey Sauce	58
Goat Cheese-stuffed Chicken Wrapped in Prosciutto	61
Pan-seared Duck Breast with Beetroot Purée	62
Cobh Seafood Pie	65
Pan-seared Cod with Seaweed Butter	66
Pan-seared Salmon with Dill & Caper Sauce	68
Roasted Cauliflower Steaks	70
Roasted Cauliflower & Couscous Salad	71
Grilled Halloumi With Courgettes & Tomatoes	73

*Opposite page (clockwise, from top left): KYTELERS INN, Kilkenny, Margaret M. Johnson; IRISH STEW, Ppy2010ha/Dreamstime;
T. CRONIN & SONS, Killarney, Co. Kerry, David M. Cisilino/Dreamstime; BUNRATTY FOLK PARK, Co. Clare, Margaret M. Johnson*

LOIN OF LAMB WITH PARSLEY & MINT SAUCE

Serves 2

Have you heard that sheep and Ireland go hand in hand or that sheep actually outnumber people? Can you imagine traveling throughout the country without seeing the woolly creatures in some of the most unimaginable places—clinging to mountains, teetering on seaside cliffs, sitting contentedly on the side of the road, or walking leisurely right down the middle! Their unique diet of wild grasses, heather, and herbs contributes to lamb with remarkable flavor and to farmers from Dingle to Donegal and Cork to Connemara claiming theirs is the best. Rub this boneless loin with a simple mix of parsley, olive oil, salt, and pepper and then add some zing at serving time with chimichurri, a thick herb sauce as common in Argentina as HP sauce is in Ireland. Serve the lamb with potatoes dauphinoise (page 90), if you wish.

For the Lamb:
- 2 tablespoons minced fresh flat-leaf parsley
- 2 tablespoons extra virgin olive oil
- Salt
- Ground black pepper
- One (8 to 10 ounces) boneless lamb loin

1. Preheat the oven to 425°F.
2. In a small bowl, combine the parsley, olive oil, salt, and pepper. Rub the mixture all over the lamb; place on a rack in a baking dish.
3. Roast the lamb, turning once, for 15 to 20 minutes or until the internal temperature reaches 135°F on an instant-read thermometer (for medium-rare).
4. Remove the lamb to a cutting board to rest for at least 5 minutes before cutting into 1/2-inch-thick slices.

For the Sauce:
- 5 tablespoons roughly chopped fresh flat-leaf parsley
- 3 tablespoons roughly chopped fresh mint
- 3 tablespoons extra virgin olive oil
- 1 teaspoon minced garlic
- 1 teaspoon lemon zest
- 1/4 teaspoon salt
- 1/2 teaspoon fresh lemon juice

For the Sauce (cont.)

1. In a small food processor, combine parsley, vinegar, garlic, oregano, and red pepper flakes; process until nearly smooth.
2. Transfer to a small saucepan over medium heat; stir in the lemon juice. Cook for 4 to 5 minutes or until warm.
3. To serve, arrange the lamb on serving plates; spoon the sauce on top.

CHIMICHURRI
Makes 3/4 cup

- 1/4 cup coarsely chopped fresh flat-leaf parsley
- 3 tablespoons red wine vinegar
- 4 garlic cloves, chopped
- 1 tablespoon fresh oregano leaves
- 2 teaspoons red pepper flakes
- 1/2 cup extra virgin olive oil

1. In a food processor, combine parsley, vinegar, garlic, oregano, and red pepper flakes; process until nearly smooth.
2. Scrape into a medium bowl; stir in oil.
3. Let stand for about 30 minutes. (It can be refrigerated in an airtight container for up to 1 week; return to room temperature before serving).

LAMB CHOPS WITH HONEY, APRICOT, & TARRAGON SAUCE

Serves 4

THE sweet-and-spicy blend of apricots and tarragon is perfect in this simple sauce for grilled or broiled lamb. The recipe was offered to me in the late 1990s from Chef Gerry Galvin, whom some call the "father of modern Irish cooking." From Kinsale, County Cork, where he nudged the town into gourmet greatness; to Moycullen, County Galway, where he relocated to Drimcong House, his name and reputation are legendary. Galvin, who passed away in 2013, suggested you serve the chops with potato, parsnip, and apple purée (page 80), a great alternatives to mashed potatoes. You might also enjoy them with celeriac mash (page 79).

- 2/3 cup (4 ounces) finely chopped dried apricots
- 2 cups canned low-salt chicken broth
- 2 tablespoons chopped fresh tarragon
- 2 1/2 tablespoons honey
- 2 teaspoons fresh lemon juice
- Salt
- Ground black pepper
- 1 teaspoon hot curry paste
- 2 tablespoons extra virgin olive oil
- 12 lamb chops
- Fresh tarragon sprigs, for garnish

1. In a small bowl, combine the apricots, chicken stock, and tarragon; let soak for at least 3 hours.
2. Transfer to the bowl of a food processor. Add 1 teaspoon of the honey, the lemon juice, salt, and pepper; process until smooth.
3. Transfer to a small saucepan over medium heat. Cook for 4 to 5 minutes or until heated through.
4. Preheat a gas grill, light a charcoal fire, or use a grill pan.
5. In a small bowl, combine the remaining honey, curry paste, and olive oil. Brush over both sides of the lamb; season with salt and pepper.
6. Grill lamb for 3 minutes on each side (for rare) and up to 8 minutes for well done.
7. To serve, arrange three chops on a serving plate; spoon the sauce on top. Garnish with tarragon sprigs.

IRISH STEW

Serves 4 to 6

For centuries, the principal cooking utensils in Irish country cottages were the iron pot and black iron skillet, both of which have been used in various forms since the time of the Celts. The pot was filled with water; and whatever meat, grain, or vegetable that was available was added for day-long cooking. Usually, the meat was kid or mutton, but bacon was often added for additional flavor. Today, lamb is the meat of choice in Ireland's national dish; and the recipe has spawned interesting variations that use lamb shanks instead of lamb cubes, turnips instead of carrots, and stout instead of stock. Most agree, however, that this recipe leans toward the classic version.

- 2 tablespoons canola oil
- 2 1/4 bone-in lamb shoulders, cut into 1/2-inch pieces
- 2 large onions, sliced
- 2 to 3 large carrots, sliced
- 1 small turnip, cut into 1-inch pieces
- 2 to 3 large russet potatoes, peeled and thickly sliced
- Salt
- Ground black pepper
- 1 tablespoon minced fresh thyme
- 2 tablespoons minced fresh flat-leaf parsley, plus more for garnish
- 1 1/2 cups lamb stock or canned low-sodium beef broth

1. Preheat the oven to 300°F.
2. In a Dutch oven, heat the oil over the medium heat.
3. Working in batches, cook the lamb on all sides for about 5 minutes or until all the meat is browned.
4. In the same pan, alternate layers of lamb, onions, carrots, turnip, and potatoes, ending with potatoes. Sprinkle each layer with salt, pepper, thyme, and some of the parsley.
5. Add the stock or broth; cover tightly with a lid.
6. Cook in the oven for 2 to 2 1/2 hours or until the meat and vegetables are tender and the stock has thickened. (Check the dish occasionally, adding more stock or broth if necessary).
7. To serve, ladle the stew into shallow bowls; sprinkle with the remaining parsley.

SHEPHERD'S PIE WITH CHEDDAR CRUST

Serves 6

More lamb, please! This time, minced lamb is the main ingredient in this traditional "pie" with a potato crust. Often made with leftover meat and potatoes from a Sunday roast, the option of using minced lamb is now a convenience factor. Not to be confused with Cottage Pie, which is made with beef, this recipe adds a bit of cheddar cheese to the potato crust for an updated version.

- 3 tablespoons canola oil
- 2 pounds ground lamb
- 1 tablespoon butter
- 1 large onion, chopped
- 1 garlic clove, crushed
- 3 large carrots, diced
- 2 small tomatoes, peeled, seeded, and chopped
- 2 tablespoons tomato paste
- 1 1/2 tablespoons flour
- 1 cup homemade beef stock or canned low-sodium beef broth
- 1 tablespoon chopped fresh thyme
- 1 tablespoon minced fresh flat-leaf parsley
- Salt
- Ground black pepper
- 3 cups mashed potatoes, for topping
- 1 cup grated cheddar cheese, for topping

1. Preheat the oven to 350°F. Coat an ovenproof baking dish with butter flavor no-stick baking spray.

2. In a Dutch oven, heat the oil over medium heat.

3. Working in batches, cook the lamb for 5 to 7 minutes or until all the meat is browned. With a slotted spoon, transfer the meat to a large bowl; discard the fat.

4. Return the pan to medium heat; and melt the butter. Add the onion, garlic, and carrots; cook for 3 to 5 minutes or until soft but not browned.

5. Stir in the tomatoes, tomato paste, and flour.

6. Stir in the broth, thyme, and parsley, scraping up the browned bits from the bottom of the pan.

7. Stir in the lamb.

8. Reduce the heat. Simmer, stirring occasionally, for 10 to 15 minutes, or until the mixture thickens. Season with salt and pepper.

9. Spoon the mixture into the prepared dish.

10. In a medium bowl, stir together the mashed potatoes and half the cheese. Spread or pipe the potatoes over the meat mixture; sprinkle the remaining cheese on top.

11. Bake for 25 to 30 minutes or until the top is browned and the filling is bubbling. Serve immediately.

Hiphoto/Dreamstime

FILET OF BEEF WITH IRISH WHISKEY SAUCE

Serves 4

IRISH grass-fed beef—a term that translates to natural, healthy, and premium—is among the finest in the world. To gain this designation, the diet of the animal is composed of a minimum of 90 percent grass or grass forage, and it must graze in open pastures for an average of more than two hundred days a year during its lifetime. A "grass-fed" eye filet, also called a "tenderloin" or "filet mignon," is the crème de la crème of steaks: it's the most tender cut of beef, the leanest cut of beef, and the one most often described as "melt in your mouth." It's also the simplest to cook, loves a good sauce on top, and welcomes any potato dish, especially champ (page 77) or colcannon (page 78), served as a side.

For the Beef:

- Four (8 ounces) beef tenderloin steaks
- Salt
- Ground black pepper
- 2 tablespoons butter
- 2 teaspoons extra virgin olive oil
- Ground mixed peppercorns, for topping

1. Season the steaks on both sides with salt and pepper.
2. In a large skillet (cast-iron preferred) over high heat, heat the butter and oil.
3. Add the seasoned steaks; cook for 2 to 3 minutes on each side.
4. Reduce the heat to medium-high; cook steaks for another 2 minutes. Turn; cook for another 2 minutes or until an instant-read thermometer inserted into the center registers 120°F (for rare) or 125°F for medium.
5. Transfer steaks to a warm platter; cover loosely with foil to allow the juices to seal.

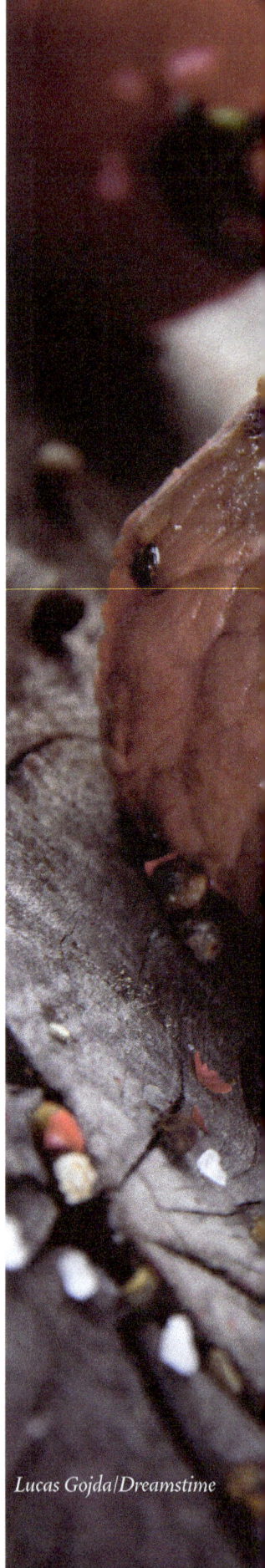

Lucas Gojda/Dreamstime

For the Sauce:

- 1 tablespoon canola oil
- 1 tablespoon butter
- 3 tablespoons finely chopped shallots
- 1/4 cup Irish whiskey
- 1/2 cup canned low-sodium beef broth
- 1/2 teaspoon Worcestershire sauce
- 2 teaspoons Dijon mustard
- 1/2 cup heavy whipping cream

1. Return the skillet to medium heat; heat the oil and butter.

2. Add the shallots; cook for 1 to 2 minutes or until soft but not browned.

3. Add the whiskey; stir with a wooden spoon, scraping up any browned bits from the bottom of the pan.

4. Add broth and Worcestershire sauce; increase heat to medium-high. Bring mixture to a boil. Whisk in mustard and cream.

5. Continue to boil, stirring frequently, for 3 to 5 minutes or until the sauce thickens; season with salt and pepper. Stir in the lemon juice.

6. To serve, transfer the steaks to serving plates; sprinkle with mixed peppercorns. Serve with the sauce.

Peteer/Dreamstime

GOAT CHEESE-STUFFED CHICKEN WRAPPED IN PROSCIUTTO

Serves 2

Blue Bell Falls Goat Cheese is produced near Charleville, County Cork, from milk that comes from a mix of breeds—white Saanen and brown Toggenburg goats from Switzerland and black and white British Alpine goats. They graze happily in picture-perfect fields outside the cheesemaking facility, enjoying a diet of lush grass and wild shrubs that infuse their milk with the perfect balance of richness and taste—to say nothing of how charming they are! The O'Sullivan family, with Breda as cheesemaker-in-charge, make plain and flavored (garlic, honey, and thyme) soft goat cheese, either one of which is perfect for stuffing these chicken breasts. (Alternately, use your favorite brand of goat cheese). Wrap them in prosciutto for an elegant meal.

- 2 boneless, skinless chicken breasts
- Salt
- Ground black pepper
- 4 ounces goat cheese, plain or flavored
- 2 teaspoons fresh thyme leaves, plus 2 to 3 sprigs, for garnish
- 2 teaspoons chopped flat-leaf parsley
- 4 slices prosciutto
- 8 ounces vine tomatoes
- 4 shallots, peeled and cut in half
- Extra virgin olive oil, for drizzling

1. Preheat the oven to 375°F. Split the chicken breasts almost in half from one long side, open out. With a rolling pin or meat mallet, flatten out the breast. Season both sides with salt and pepper.
2. Spread half the goat cheese on each piece of chicken; sprinkle with the thyme and parsley.
3. Fold the chicken over to enclose the cheese; wrap each one in two slices of the prosciutto.
4. Lightly oil a shallow ovenproof dish. Place the chicken in the dish; surround with tomatoes and shallots. Drizzle with olive oil; sprinkle with salt and pepper. Top with thyme sprigs.
5. Bake for 30 to 35 minutes or until the prosciutto is crisp and an instant-read thermometer inserted into the center registers 165°F.

PAN-SEARED DUCK BREAST WITH BEETROOT PURÉE

Serves 2

Duck farming is firmly established in Ireland with at least four producers—Silverhill in County Monaghan, Feighcullen in County Kildare, Thornhill in County Cavan, and Skeaghanore in County Cork—providing fresh and oven-ready ducks to markets throughout the country. Cooking duck breast is nearly as popular with home cooks as it is with restaurant chefs, namely because it's so easy to prepare. A sweet-tart sauce, usually made of something as simple as cranberry sauce or apple chutney, is a traditional complement to the rich flavor of duck meat and its crispy skin, but beetroot purée offers a pleasant surprise. You can follow the recipe for roasted beetroot on page 38 and purée it or the one provided here that uses boiled beetroot. For another sweet complement, serve the duck with celeriac mash (page 79) or parsnip and apple purée (page 80), if you wish.

Beetroot Purée

- 1 large beetroot peeled, cooked, and cut into 8 slices
- 2 tablespoons extra virgin olive oil
- 1 teaspoon salt
- 1/2 teaspoon granulated sugar

1. In a food processor, combine the beetroot, olive oil, salt, and sugar. Process for 30 seconds, scraping down the sides of the bowl as needed; process for 30 seconds longer until smooth.
2. Transfer the mixture to a bowl; set aside.

For the Duck Breast:

- 2 boneless duck breast halves, skin on
- Salt
- Ground pepper
- 1/4 cup duck fat or canola oil

1. Preheat the oven to 425°F. With a sharp knife, score the duck skin in a diamond pattern (do not cut into flesh). Trim the breast of any excess fat.
2. Season the duck on both sides with salt and pepper.

For the Duck Breast (Cont.)

3. In an ovenproof skillet, heat the fat or oil over medium heat. Add the duck breasts, skin-side down. Cook, undisturbed, for about 5 minutes or until the skin is browned and crisp.

4. With a spatula, carefully turn over the duck breasts; cook the second side for 2 minutes longer.

5. Transfer the skillet to the oven; cook for 8 minutes longer or until a meat thermometer inserted into the center registers 130°F (for medium). Transfer the duck to a work surface; tent with foil to keep warm. Let rest for 10 minutes.

6. While the duck is resting, gently reheat the purée over medium heat.

7. To serve, spoon and spread the purée onto 2 plates. Cut the duck breast on the bias and arrange on top of the purée.

Imagesupply/Dreamstime

COBH SEAFOOD PIE

Serves 6 to 8

The charming seaside town of Cobh, historically significant as the last port of call for the *Titanic*, was originally called Queenstown in honor of Queen Victoria's 1848 visit. The first purpose-built hotel in Ireland opened there in 1854 and called itself The Queen's Hotel to commemorate her visit. It's now called The Commodore and holds court in the center of the town just a few yards from where the queen stepped ashore. It's one of the most popular places in town for visitors and locals alike, who enjoy the hospitality of its Club Café and Grille and local specialties like this creamy seafood pie.

- 8 ounces white fish, such as cod or haddock
- 8 ounces salmon
- 1 1/4 cup milk
- 8 tablespoons butter
- 1 small leek (white part only), chopped
- 1 celery stalk, chopped
- 1 carrot, chopped
- 1 garlic clove, chopped
- 1 cup fish stock
- 1 tablespoon flour
- Salt
- Ground black pepper
- 2 cups mashed potatoes, for topping

1. Preheat the oven to 350°F. Coat an ovenproof baking dish with butter flavored no-stick cooking spray.
2. In a medium saucepan, combine the fish and milk over medium-low heat. Poach the fish for 6 to 8 minutes or until it softens.
3. With a slotted spoon, transfer to a plate. Flake the fish; remove any bones. Strain the milk into a small bowl; reserve.
4. In a large saucepan over medium heat, melt 4 tablespoons of the butter. Add the onion, leek, celery, and carrot. Cook for 5 to 6 minutes or until the vegetables are soft but not browned.
5. Stir in the garlic; cook for 1 to 2 minutes longer.
6. Stir in the reserved milk, cream, and 1/2 cup of the stock. Cook, stirring continuously, until the sauce starts to thicken; stir in the flour.
7. Add remaining 1/2 cup stock and flaked fish; season with salt and pepper.
8. Spoon the mixture into the prepared dish. Spread or pipe the potatoes on top; dot with remaining 4 tablespoon butter.
9. Bake the pie for 20 to 25 minutes or until the top is browned and the filling is bubbling. Serve immediately.

PAN-SEARED COD WITH SEAWEED BUTTER

Serves 4

It's safe to say that you'll find cod, a firm white fish, on menus throughout Ireland. Simply seasoned, it can be pan-seared, roasted, or grilled. Its subtle flavor and flaky texture welcome classic sauces or toppings with strong flavors like seaweed butter. Called *beurre d'algue* in France, it's a flavorful butter compounded with dried dulse or kelp. Cooking with seaweed is gaining popularity in Ireland where you can buy a number of varieties in artisan food shops. If you wish, serve this cod, inspired by a recipe from the Winding Stair Restaurant in Dublin (pictured opposite), with boiled new potatoes, fresh or frozen peas.

For the Seaweed Butter:

- 1 ounce dried dulse or kelp flakes[1]
- 4 ounces unsalted butter, at room temperature

1. Combine the dried seaweed and butter in a food processor; pulse 8 to 10 times until smooth.
2. Use the butter immediately or refrigerate in a plastic container for 1 week; freeze for up to 3 months.

For the Cod:

- Four (5 to 6 ounces) skin-on cod fillets, about 1-inch thick
- Salt
- Ground black pepper
- 2 tablespoons extra virgin olive oil
- 4 tablespoons seaweed butter, cut into pieces
- Juice from 1/2 lemon
- 1 tablespoon minced fresh herbs, such as flat-leaf parsley and chives
- Lemon wedges, for garnish

---

[1] You can buy dried seaweed in health food stores in the U.S. or online from brands such as Maine Coast Sea Vegetables (seaveg.com) and Atlantic Sea Farms (atlanticseafarms.com).

Jitka Smolkova/The Winding Stair, Dublin

For the Cod (Cont.)

1. Sprinkle both sides of the fish with salt and pepper. In a 10- to 12-inch nonstick skillet, heat the oil over medium-high heat.

2. Once sizzling, reduce the heat to medium. Cook the fish, skin-side down, for 2 to 3 minutes or until the skin begins to crisp.

3. Add 2 tablespoons of butter to the pan around each fillet; swirl in the pan. Cook for another few minutes until the skin is crisp.

4. With a spatula, carefully turn over the fish; cook the second side for another 3 to 4 minutes or until cooked through.

5. Transfer the fish to four warmed plates.

6. Return the skillet to medium heat. Melt the remaining 2 tablespoons of butter.

7. Add the lemon juice and herbs; swirl to blend.

8. To serve, top each fish fillet with a spoonful of seaweed butter. Serve with potatoes, peas. Garnish with lemon wedges.

PAN-SEARED SALMON WITH DILL & CAPER SAUCE

Serves 2

IRISH playwright Oscar Wilde once said, "I have the simplest of tastes; I am always satisfied with the best." His comment almost seems directed at a recipe like this for a simple pan-seared salmon, one of Ireland's most treasured fishes. Serve it topped with a tasty dill and capers-rich tartar sauce, a classic sauce that goes well with most fish, and steamed or sautéed spinach. Serve the salmon with mini potato gratins (page 88), if you wish.

For the Salmon:

- Two 6-ounce salmon fillets
- Sea salt
- Ground black pepper
- 2 tablespoons canola oil
- Lemon wedges, for garnish
- Steamed spinach, for serving (optional)

1. Season both sides of the salmon with salt and pepper.
2. In an oven-proof skillet, heat the oil to sizzling; add the fish.
3. Cook, undisturbed, for 3 to 5 minutes or until golden.
4. Turn over; cook the second side for another 5 minutes. Alternately, transfer to a preheated 375°F oven and cook for 5 to 6 minutes or until the internal temperature registers 130°F on an instant-read thermometer.
5. Remove from oven; let the fish rest for 5 minutes.

Olgany/Dreamstime

For the Sauce:

- 1/2 cup mayonnaise
- 3 tablespoons pickle relish
- 1 tablespoon fresh lemon juice, plus more to taste
- 1 tablespoon capers, chopped
- 1 tablespoon chopped fresh dill
- 1/2 Worcestershire sauce
- 1/2 teaspoon Dijon mustard
- Salt
- Ground black pepper

1. In a small bowl, combine the mayonnaise, relish, lemon juice, capers, dill, Worcestershire sauce, and mustard; stir until blended. Season with salt and pepper.

2. Cover and refrigerate for at least 30 minutes or for up to 1 week.

3. To serve, transfer the salmon to serving plates. Top with the sauce; garnish with a lemon wedge. Serve with spinach, if desired.

ROASTED CAULIFLOWER STEAKS

Serves 4 to 6

In recent years, there has been a significant increase in the number of people in Ireland adopting a plant-based diet—more than ten thousand, in fact. The rise in veganism has been driven by several reasons—concerns over animal welfare, environmental sustainability, and personal health concerns—accounting for the fact that the number of vegans has more than quadrupled in the last decade. (Ireland now ranks tenth in the top countries around the world and sixth in Europe). If you visit Ireland, expect to find vegan and vegetarian options everywhere—from two-star Michelin restaurants to gastropubs and wine bars offering dishes with familiar ingredients, such as pasta, polenta, quinoa, and couscous, along with less familiar ones like freekeh (an ancient Middle Eastern wheat grain), fregola (a Sardinian food that's a cross between a grain and a pasta), and dukkah (an Egyptian mix of nuts, seeds, and warm spices).

To satisfy Ireland's ever-changing tastes, vegan and vegetarian options are nearly as widespread today as choices used to be for how you wanted your steak cooked. For this vegan cauliflower "steak," there's no need to choose! (After cutting the "steaks" from the center of each head, reserve the outer florets for the cauliflower and couscous salad recipe that follows).

For the Steaks:
- 2 large cauliflower, outer leaves removed
- 4 tablespoon extra virgin olive oil, plus more for drizzling
- Sea salt
- Ground black pepper

1. Preheat the oven to 425°F. Line two baking sheets with parchment paper.
2. Starting in the center of each cauliflower, cut two to three 1 1/2-inch-thick slices from each, leaving the core intact.
3. In a large skillet, heat 1 tablespoon olive oil over medium heat. Working in batches, sear each cauliflower steak for 2 to 3 minutes on each side or until golden. Repeat with remaining oil and steaks.
4. Transfer to the prepared pans; season both sides with salt and pepper. Drizzle with a little more olive oil.
5. Roast the cauliflower for 25 to 28 minutes or until the core of each steak is fork-tender.

For the Sauce:
- 1/2 cup pine nuts
- 1/2 cup hazelnuts, chopped
- 1 bunch fresh flat-leaf parsley, chopped
- 5 tablespoons chopped fresh mint
- 1/2 cup golden raisins, chopped
- Zest and juice of 3 lemons
- 1/2 teaspoon red pepper flakes
- 1/2 cup extra virgin olive oil

Daria Arnatova/Dreamstime

For the Sauce (Cont.)

1. In a medium bowl, combine the pine nuts, hazelnuts, parsley, raisins, lemon zest, juice, pepper flakes, and olive oil.

2. To serve, arrange the steaks on a serving plate and top with a few tablespoons of sauce (reserve remaining sauce for the couscous salad).

ROASTED CAULIFLOWER & COUSCOUS SALAD

Serves 4

- Cauliflower florets reserved from cauliflower steak
- 3 tablespoons extra virgin olive oil
- 2 teaspoons curry powder
- 1/4 teaspoon salt
- 1/4 teaspoon ground black pepper
- 2 cups cooked couscous
- 1/2 cup remaining nut mixture from cauliflower steaks
- Balsamic vinegar, for drizzling

1. Preheat the oven to 375°F. Line a baking sheet with parchment paper.

2. In a large bowl, toss the reserved cauliflower florets with oil, curry powder, salt, and pepper.

3. Spread out on the prepared pan. Roast, turning once or twice, for 25 to 30 minutes or until slightly charred and tender (do not overcook).

4. Combine the couscous and 1/4 to 1/2 cup of the remaining nut mixture in a bowl; toss well.

5. To serve, spoon the couscous mixture onto four plates; arrange the cauliflower florets on top. Season with salt and pepper; drizzle with balsamic vinegar.

Ingrid Balabanova/Dreamstime

GRILLED HALLOUMI WITH COURGETTES & TOMATOES

Serves 4

If halloumi sounds like it has no place in an Irish cookbook, think again! For the uninitiated, halloumi is a layered, brined white cheese with a slightly spongy texture and tangy/salty taste. The rindless cheese is traditionally made from a combination of goat and sheep milk on the island of Cyprus. It's sometimes made from cow's milk; but since 2009, Irish farmer Johnny Lynch has been making the Cypriot-styled cheese with milk from his herd of buffaloes in Macroom, County Cork (for more on the Macroom Buffalo Farm, see page 32). The cheese has a high heating point, so it's great for grilling, baking, or broiling. The cheese is suitable for vegetarians and has quickly gained in popularity served with grains or, as in this recipe, with grilled courgettes (the Irish call zucchini by its French name), cherry tomatoes, and wild mushrooms.

- 3 tablespoons extra virgin olive oil
- Zest and juice of 1 lemon
- 8 ounces halloumi, cut into 1/4-inch-thick slices
- 1 teaspoon salt
- 1/2 teaspoon ground black pepper
- 2 medium courgettes, cut lengthwise into 1/4-inch-thick slices
- 8 to 10 cremini mushrooms
- 8 to 10 cherry tomatoes
- Fresh flat-leaf parsley, for garnish
- Rosemary sprigs, for garnish

1. Heat a grill pan over medium-high heat.
2. In a small bowl, whisk together the olive oil, lemon zest, and juice; brush some on both sides of the halloumi slices.
3. Stir the salt and pepper into the remaining lemon oil; brush it on the courgette slices and mushrooms.
4. Grill the halloumi for 2 to 3 minutes on each side or until it has grill marks.
5. Grill the courgette slices for 3 to 4 minutes on each side until tender.
6. Cook the mushrooms for 1 to 2 minutes or until lightly browned.
7. To serve, arrange the grilled courgettes, grilled mushrooms, and tomatoes on four serving plates; top with two slices of halloumi. Garnish with parsley and rosemary.

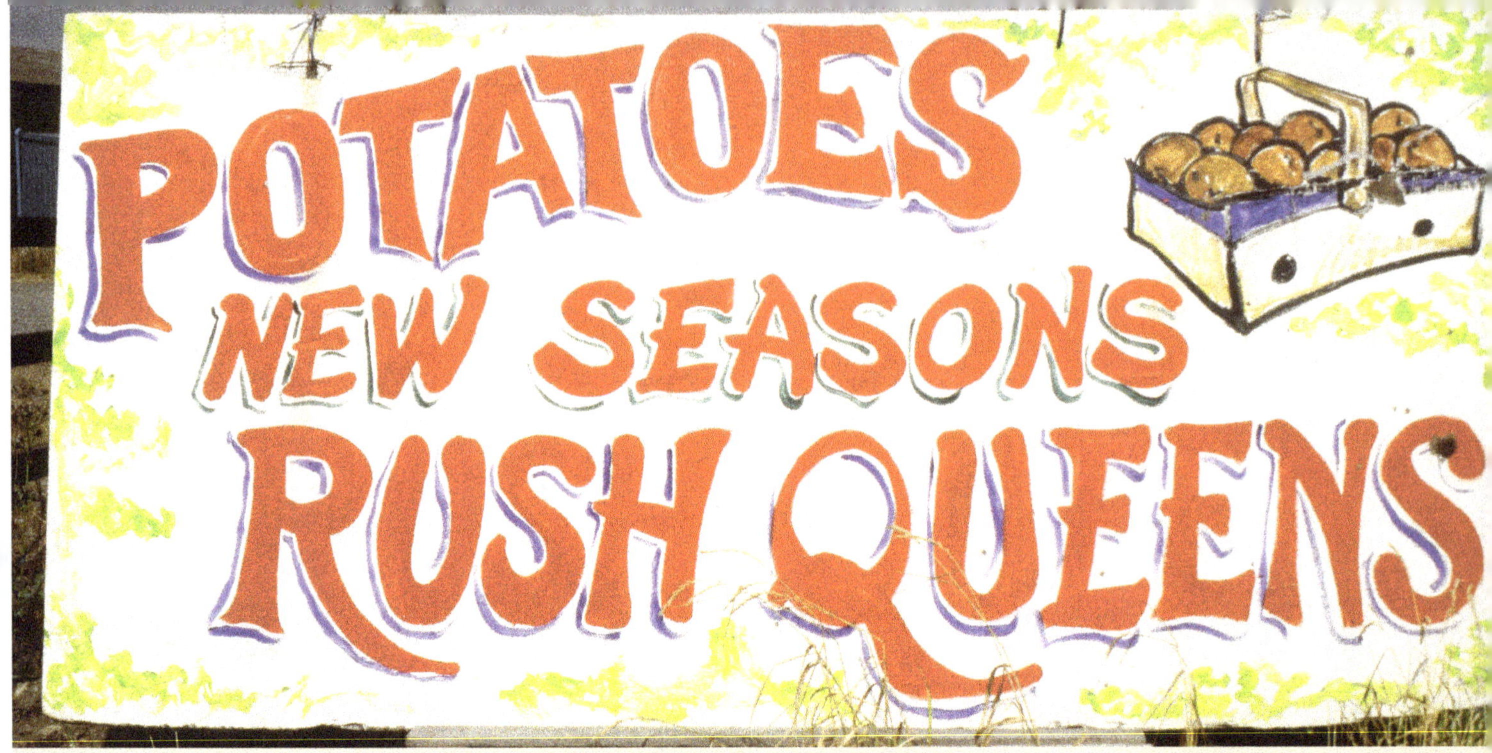
POTATOES
NEW SEASONS
RUSH QUEENS

THE NATURAL HEALTH FOOD
HIGH FIBRE • HIGH QUALITY
IRISH GARDEN POTATOES
LOW FAT • LOW CALORIES
ROOSTER
NET WEIGHT 10 kg

GOLDEN
WONDER

ROOSTER
ROOSTER
ROOSTER

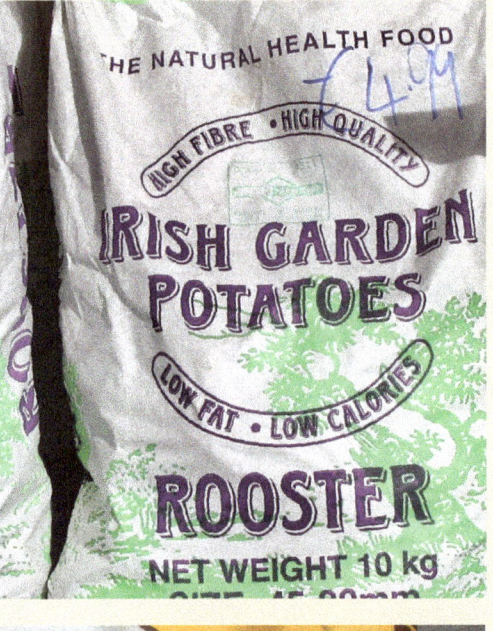

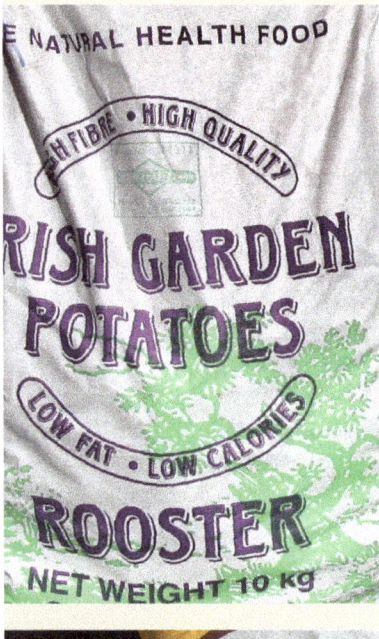

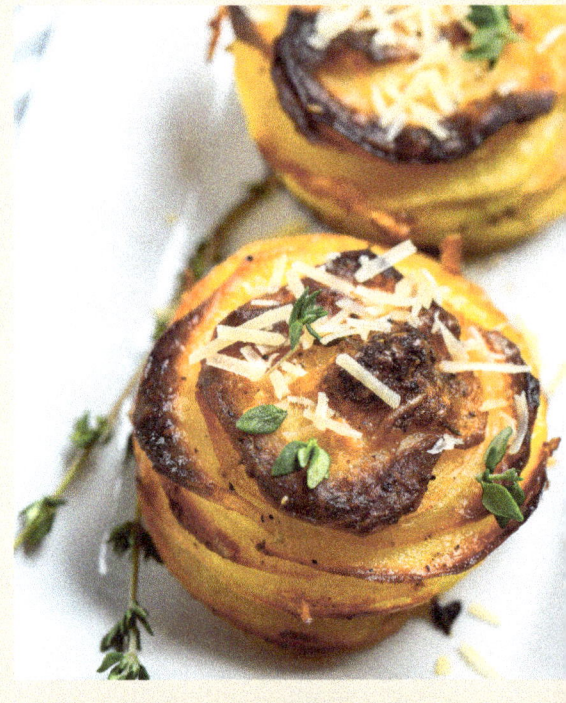

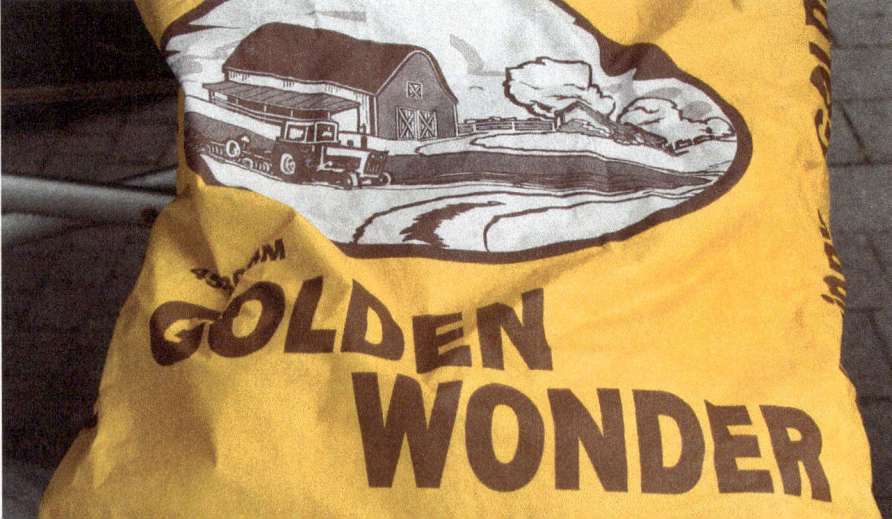

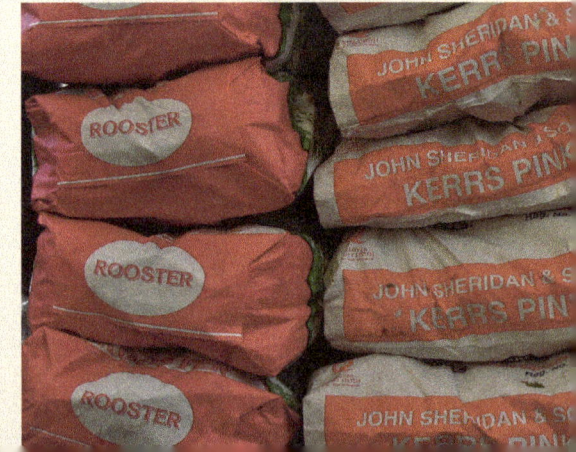

CHAPTER 3

SIDES
Mash & More

Champ	77
Colcannon	78
Celeriac Mash	79
Potato, Parsnip, & Apple Purée	80
Boxty	83
Blue Cheese Potato Cakes	84
Three-cheese Rösti	86
Mini Potato Gratins	88
Dauphinoise Potatoes	90
The Great Potato Debate	91

Opposite page (clockwise, from top): RUSH, Co. Fingal, Margaret M. Johnson; MINI POTATO GRATINS, Sriba3/Dreamstime; TEMPLE BAR MARKET, Dublin, Margaret M. Johnson; MIDLETON FARMERS MARKET, Co. Cork, Margaret M. Johnson; GALWAY FARMERS MARKET, Galway, Margaret M. Johnson

CHAMP

Serves 4

ONCE potatoes were introduced to Ireland at the end of the sixteenth century, the country's moist, mild climate and rich soil made them a natural crop and one that was easily cultivated year-round on even the smallest piece of land. Millions of Irish "cottiers," farmers huddling as renters on the tiny strips of land they tilled, subsisted exclusively on potatoes; and it's been estimated that the average peasant family consumed ten pounds of potatoes a day and sometimes managed for an entire year on a one-acre yield. The Irish eventually became totally dependent on the potato, which provided a remarkably healthy and economical diet when supplemented by oatmeal and dairy products. Champ, sometimes called "poundies," is a traditional mashed potato dish especially associated with Northern Ireland. Served in a mound with a well of melted butter in the center, it's traditionally eaten with a spoon, starting from the outside of the mound.

- 1 1/2 pounds russet potatoes, peeled and cut into 2-inch pieces
- 1 1/4 cups milk
- 6 tablespoons butter
- 1 1/3 cups chopped fresh chives or scallions
- Salt
- Ground black pepper

1. In a large saucepan, cook the potatoes in boiling salted water for 18 to 20 minutes or until tender. Drain and mash.
2. In a saucepan large enough to hold the cooked potatoes, combine the milk and 4 tablespoons of the butter over medium heat.
3. When the butter melts, add the chives; reduce heat to simmer. Cook 2 to 4 minutes longer or until the chives soften.
4. Stir in the potatoes, salt, and pepper until blended.
5. To serve, spoon champ into a deep bowl. Make a well in the center; top with remaining butter.

Olga Kriger / Dreamstime

COLCANNON

Serves 4 to 6

MANY traditional dishes are associated with festivals and feast days from both the Celtic calendar of the druids and the newer Christian calendar. Colcannon (from the Irish *cal ceann fhionn*, or "white-headed cabbage"), a mashed potato dish flavored with kale or cabbage, is the main dish of the Halloween (All Hallow's Eve) dinner. Its origins may lie in the need to use up the last leafy vegetables in the fall garden. In keeping with tradition, a carefully wrapped gold ring is placed in one of the bowls, and the diner who finds it is likely to marry within the coming year. While a true colcannon is made with cooked, finely chopped kale, cabbage is also used.

- 1 pound russet potatoes, peeled and cut into 2-inch pieces
- 1 pound cabbage, cored, quartered, and shredded
- 1/2 cup milk, plus more if needed
- 3 tablespoons butter, plus more for topping
- Salt
- Ground black pepper

1. In a medium saucepan, cook the potatoes in boiling salted water for 15 to 20 minutes or until tender. Drain and mash.

2. In another medium saucepan, cook the cabbage in boiling salted water for 5 to 7 minutes or until tender. Drain.

3. Stir the cabbage into the potatoes. Return the pan to low heat; stir in the milk, butter, salt, and pepper.

4. Cook until heated through, adding more milk if needed.

5. Serve immediately, topped with additional butter, if desired.

CELERIAC MASH

Serves 4

Celeriac is simply a celery root, a knobby-looking root vegetable that's having quite a moment in Irish cooking. It has an earthy flavor that pairs well with potatoes, both in texture and flavor.

- 1 1/4 pounds celeriac, peeled and cut into 1-inch pieces
- 1 1/4 pounds russet potatoes, peeled and cut into 1-inch pieces
- 1/4 cup heavy whipping cream
- 2 tablespoons butter
- Salt
- Ground black pepper

1. In a large saucepan, cook the celeriac in boiling salted water for 15 minutes.

2. Add the potatoes; boil for 15 minutes longer or until tender. Drain and mash.

3. Return the pan to low heat; stir in the cream, butter, salt, and pepper. Cook until heated through, adding more cream, if needed.

4. Serve immediately, topped with additional butter, if desired.

Mallivan | Depositphotos

POTATO, PARSNIP, & APPLE PURÉE

Serves 6 to 8

ALTHOUGH potatoes are the food frequently associated with Ireland and its people, there are other vegetables grown there from early times. "The Irish feed much upon parsnip," a historian wrote in 1673; and in most Irish households, they feed on cabbage, onions, and cauliflower as well, with turnips (also known as swede or rutabaga) thrown in for good measure. As with most foods that seem to have a national identity, climate and growing conditions often determine what's eaten; so root vegetables, with their excellent keeping qualities, are also Irish favorites. Two of Ireland's most popular vegetables combine with apples in this delicious purée, a nearly perfect accompaniment to poultry and lamb.

- 2 pounds of parsnips (peeled and sliced)
- 2 pounds of russet potatoes (peeled and chopped)
- 1/2 cup of water
- 3 Granny Smith apples (peeled, cored, and cubed)
- 1 cup warm milk
- 8 tablespoons butter

1. Cook parsnips and potatoes in a large saucepan of salted boiling water for 20 to 25 minutes or until tender. Drain and mash. Return to the saucepan off the heat.

2. In a medium saucepan over low heat, combine water and apples. Cover; simmer for 20 to 25 minutes or until tender.

3. Drain and mash. Stir into the potato and parsnip mixture.

4. Stir in milk (add more if needed) and butter.

5. With a handheld mixer or immersion blender, blend until smooth.

6. Stir over medium heat until heated through. Season with salt and pepper. (You can prepare this in advance and reheat.)

Mkoudis | Dreamstime

BOXTY

Serves 4

Boxty, a popular potato cake, is an authentic dish and one of Ireland's most popular traditional foods. Dating to the 1700s, it's traditionally associated with the North Midlands, North Connacht, and Southern Ulster, particularly counties Leitrim, Mayo, Sligo, Donegal, and Cavan. Many believe boxty was originally a peasant dish, but there's more evidence to suggest it was a celebratory meal that brought joy to those who made it—so much so that it inspired rhymes, poetry, songs, stories, and folklore and became a valued aspect of Irish culture.

Many recipes for boxty exist, including some made with mashed potatoes alone, some made with combination of grated raw and mashed potatoes, and even some made with grated celeriac. McNiffe's Bakery and Dromod, both in County Leitrim, commercially produce the popular vegan-friendly version (100 percent plant-based) in cakes, loaves, and pan boxty with just three simple ingredients—potatoes, flour, and a sprinkle of salt. These boxty varieties are nearly crepe-like in thinness and used as part of an Irish breakfast, in cheese toasties, or simply spread with butter. As an accompaniment to meat, poultry, or fish, try one of these heartier versions.

- 1 medium waxy potato, such as Yukon Gold, peeled and grated
- 1 cup flour
- 2 teaspoons salt
- 2 teaspoons baking powder
- 1 cup mashed potatoes
- 2 eggs, lightly beaten
- 1/4 cup milk, plus more if needed
- Canola oil, for frying

1. Place the grated potato into a clean cloth; squeeze to remove excess moisture.
2. In a medium bowl, whisk together the flour, salt, and baking powder.
3. Combine the flour mixture with the raw potatoes, mashed potatoes, and eggs. Add enough milk to make a thick batter.
4. In a large skillet over medium heat, heat 2 to 3 tablespoons of oil. Working in batches, drop a heaping tablespoon of the potato mixture into the hot pan. Cook for about 4 minutes on each side, or until golden brown. (Cakes can be prepared up to this point, placed on a baking sheet, and reheated in a 250°F oven for about 5 minutes).

BLUE CHEESE POTATO CAKES

Makes 12

The recipe for these crispy potato cakes comes, once again, from Denis Cotter, the chef-proprietor of Paradiso, his vegetarian restaurant in Cork (see page 36). Laced with a healthy amount of Tipperary-made Cashel Blue Cheese (imported by the Kerrygold brand), he would generally serve them with a flageolet bean dish or a vegetable stew, but non-vegetarians love them served with meat or fish.

- 1 1/2 pounds russet potatoes, peeled and cut into 2-inch pieces
- 2 tablespoons butter, melted
- 2 tablespoons chopped fresh chives
- 2 tablespoons minced fresh dill
- 2 tablespoons minced fresh flat-leaf parsley
- 1/4 teaspoon nutmeg
- Salt
- Ground black pepper
- 4 ounces crumbled Cashel Blue cheese
- 1 egg yolk
- Flour, for dredging
- 2 eggs beaten with 1/2 cup milk, for egg wash
- Breadcrumbs, for dredging
- Vegetable oil, for frying
- Sour cream or crème fraîche, for serving

1. In a large saucepan, cook the potatoes over medium heat in boiling salted water for 18 to 20 minutes or until tender; drain and mash.

2. Stir in the butter, chives, dill, parsley, and nutmeg; mix well. Season with salt and pepper. Let cool completely.

3. Stir in the cheese and egg yolk. (The cheese should remain in uneven crumbled lumps scattered through the potatoes.)

4. Shape the potato mixture into 12 cakes; refrigerate for 30 minutes to firm.

5. Lightly dredge in flour; coat with egg wash; coat with breadcrumbs.

6. In a large skillet, heat 2 to 3 tablespoons of oil over medium-high heat. Working in batches, cook the cakes for 3 to 5 minutes on each side or until browned and crisp. (Cakes can be prepared up to this point, placed on a baking sheet, and reheated in a 250°F oven for about 5 minutes).

7. Serve with a dollop of sour cream or crème fraîche.

Bhofack2 | Dreamstime

THREE-CHEESE RÖSTI

Serves 4

A "kissing cousin" to boxty, rösti is a popular Swiss potato dish whose name translates to "crisp and golden." It was originally a breakfast dish commonly eaten by farmers in the German-speaking canton of Bern; but it's now eaten all over *Switzerland*, and many Swiss people consider rösti to be a national dish. Unlike boxty, rösti is made only with shredded potatoes (generally boiled and left to chill overnight before shredding) and fried as one large cake in lots of butter until golden brown. Bord Bia, the Irish Food Board, offers its seal of approval on the dish and shares several recipes for it, including this three-cheese rösti that makes a wonderful side dish or light lunch. For best results, chill the potatoes overnight.

- 16 ounces waxy potatoes, such as Yukon Gold
- 2 ounces cream cheese, cut into small pieces
- 2 ounces mozzarella, diced and coarsely grated
- 2 ounces washed rind cheese, such as brie, cut into small pieces
- Sea salt
- Ground black pepper
- 3 tablespoons butter
- 2 tablespoons canola oil
- Sour cream or crème fraîche, for serving
- Mixed greens, for garnish (optional)

1. In a large saucepan, cook the potatoes over medium heat in boiling salted water for 18 to 20 minutes or until just tender but not soft. Drain; cool. Chill for at least 3 hours, preferably overnight.

2. In a small bowl, beat the cream cheese, mozzarella, and brie until just combined.

3. Peel the potatoes. Using the large holes of a box grater, grate the potatoes into a mixing bowl. Season with salt and pepper.

4. In a 10-inch nonstick skillet over medium-high heat, heat 2 tablespoons of the butter and 1 tablespoon of the oil until hot.

5. Add half the potatoes. With the back of a spoon, press the potatoes into a 1-inch-thick round to cover the bottom of the pan. Cook for 4 to 5 minutes or until the potatoes begin to brown on the bottom.

6. Reduce the heat to very low; spoon on the cheese mixture. With a pallet knife, spread the cheese to within 1 inch of the edge of the potatoes.

7. Cover with the remaining potatoes, pressing down and around to cover the cheese mixture. Continue to cook for 5 to 6 minutes longer or until the rösti is browned and crisp on the bottom.

8. Gently shake the pan or use a spatula to loosen the rösti; carefully slide it onto a plate.

9. Add the remaining oil and butter; heat until the butter melts.

10. Return the rösti to the pan, uncooked side down. Cook for another 8 to 10 minutes or until the potatoes are crisp and golden and the cheese begins to ooze out (adjust heat as necessary to promote even browning and to prevent scorching).

11. Loosen again; slide back onto the plate. Let cool for 5 minutes before cutting into wedges. Serve with sour cream or crème fraîche and mixed greens, if desired.

Bord Bia/Irish Food Board

MINI POTATO GRATINS

Makes 12

THESE individual potatoes are show-stoppers with steaks, chops, and roasts. They require a little more effort in assembly, but they're well worth it for their cheesy taste and lovely presentation—they also reheat beautifully if you have any left over.

- 3 medium russet potatoes, peeled and thinly sliced
- 3 tablespoons butter, melted
- 2 tablespoons extra virgin olive oil
- 1 garlic clove, minced
- 1 tablespoon chopped fresh thyme, plus more for garnish
- 1 teaspoon salt
- 1/4 teaspoon ground black pepper, plus more for sprinkling
- 3 ounces grated Swiss cheese, such as the Kerrygold brand, plus more for sprinkling
- 1/2 cup heavy whipping cream

1. Preheat the oven to 375°F. Coat a standard muffin pan with butter flavor no-stick cooking spray.

2. In a large bowl, toss the potatoes with the butter, olive oil, garlic, thyme, salt, and pepper; stir to coat. Add half the cheese; toss again.

3. Layer the potato slices evenly into each muffin cup, filling to the top. Pour some of the cream over each cup. Sprinkle remaining cheese on top.

4. Bake the gratins, rotating the pan halfway through, for 30 to 35 minutes or until the potatoes are golden brown and crisp on top and tender when pierced with the tip of a sharp knife.

5. Let cool for 5 minutes. Run a knife around the side of the cups to loosen. Serve immediately; garnish with thyme and a few grinds of black pepper.

DAUPHINOISE POTATOES

Serves 8

THE term "gratin" refers to a dish of layered vegetables, most often potatoes, and cheese. Born before the French Revolution in the southeastern province of Dauphin, *Gratin Dauphinoise* is now a dish known worldwide and adaptable to many types of cheese. It was typically served during great feasts and celebrations in France, perhaps because of its elegant presentation and flavor, some of which comes from the addition of garlic. Adding garlic to foods is actually nothing new in Ireland, and there are now some farms given over exclusively to growing several heritage varieties: Drummond House in County Louth, White Gold Irish Garlic in County Kildare, and West Cork Garlic in County Cork, to name a few.

- 2 1/4 cups heavy whipping cream
- 2 1/4 cups milk
- 3 garlic cloves
- 8 large russet potatoes, peeled and thinly sliced
- Salt
- Ground black pepper
- 4 ounces grated Swiss cheese, such as the Kerrygold brand

1. Preheat the oven to 375°F. Coat an ovenproof gratin dish with butter flavor no-stick cooking spray.

2. In a large saucepan, bring the cream, milk, and garlic to simmer over medium heat.

3. Stir in the potatoes. Cook, stirring gently to prevent sticking, for 8 to 10 minutes or until nearly tender when pierced with the tip of a sharp knife.

4. With a slotted spoon, transfer the potatoes to the prepared dish. Pour the cream over the potatoes, discarding garlic. Season with salt and pepper; sprinkle with the cheese.

5. Bake for 50 to 55 minutes or until the potatoes are tender and the top is browned and crisp.

Margaret M. Johnson

THE GREAT POTATO DEBATE

While there's no debate on the popularity of potatoes as an authentic Irish food, there's considerable debate on how they arrived there. Some historians claim that Sir Walter Raleigh planted the first potato in Europe in 1585 in a garden in Myrtle Grove, his gabled Elizabethan mansion in Youghal (pronounced yawl) in East Cork. Raleigh was granted Irish lands by Queen Elizabeth I for his help in putting down the Desmond Rebellion of 1579 and served as the mayor, or warder, of Youghal in 1588. Others claim that Raleigh first showed his New World discovery to Queen Elizabeth, who reportedly exclaimed, "It's a tuber, it's ugly, give it to the Irish!"

Another story says the potato was introduced to Europe as a result of Sir Francis Drake's voyage to South America where the potato had been cultivated by the Incas for centuries; others believe the potato was swept ashore from the wrecks of the Spanish Armada along the coast of Ireland.

Whichever story, if any, is true, the potato has been a mainstay of Irish cuisine for centuries. For generations, the Irish were totally dependent on this vegetable, which proved to be a remarkably healthy and economical foodstuff when supplemented by oatmeal and dairy products. By the early 1600s, the potato was Ireland's major crop; and it continued as such until September 1845, when the potato blight appeared in Counties Waterford and Wexford. By the next summer, the blight had swept Ireland. The Great Hunger had begun.

CHAPTER 4

SWEETS
Puddings, Tarts, Crumbles, & Cakes

Laughter is brightest in the place where the food is.
—Irish Proverb

Bread & Butter Pudding with Whiskey & Caramel Sauce	94
Sticky Toffee Pudding	96
Honeycomb	97
Summer Pudding	99
Sticky Pear & Ginger Cake	100
Buffalo Ricotta & Berry Tart	102
Coffee & Walnut Cake	104
Fallen Chocolate Cake with Brown Bread Ice Cream	106
Irish Apple Cake	109
Blood Orange & Polenta Cakes	110
Lemon Loaf with Rosemary Drizzle	112
Lemon Posset with Blueberry Compote	115
Pear, Apricot, & Almond Roulade	117
Profiteroles with Chocolate Sauce	118
Rhubarb & Elderflower Crumble	121
Shortbread	122
The Cheese Course	125

Opposite page (clockwise, from top left): COTTAGE & GARDEN, Adare, Co. Limerick, Margaret M. Johnson; APPLE CRUMBLE, Christine Mehedinteanu/Dreamstime; PUDDING IN TEACUP, Zdenek Dolezel/Dreamstime; MIKEY RYAN'S PUB, Cashel, Co. Tipperary, Margaret M. Johnson; BLUEBERRY MOUSSE, Bellaruslady/Dreamstime

BREAD AND BUTTER PUDDING WITH WHISKEY & CARAMEL SAUCE

Serves 10

EVEN devoted Irish cooks have discovered that traditional bread and butter pudding can be made with several other breads—including panettone, barmbrack, croissants, or a baguette—and baked full size or in ramekins for individual service. This recipe uses a loaf of buttery, rich brioche and adds a touch of Irish whiskey for flavor and a handful of pecans for crunch. Start the pudding a day ahead to let the bread absorb the custard. You can make the caramel sauce one day ahead or cook it while the pudding bakes.

For the Pudding:

- One 16-ounce loaf brioche, cut into 1/2-inch cubes
- 8 tablespoons unsalted butter, melted
- 1 1/2 cups sugar
- 5 large eggs
- 4 cups heavy whipping cream
- 1/4 teaspoon salt
- 3 tablespoons Irish whiskey
- 1 teaspoon vanilla bean paste
- 1 cup chopped pecans

1. In a large bowl, toss the bread with the melted butter.
2. In another large bowl, beat the sugar and eggs with an electric mixer on medium speed for about 3 minutes or until light and fluffy.
3. Add the cream and salt; beat until smooth.
4. Stir in the whiskey and vanilla bean paste.
5. Pour the egg mixture over the bread; toss to coat.
6. Arrange the bread in a 13x9-inch glass baking dish; sprinkle with pecans. Cover with plastic wrap; refrigerate overnight.
7. Preheat the oven to 325°F. Uncover the pudding; bake for about 1 1/4 hours or until the top is browned and a skewer inserted into the center comes out clean.

For the Sauce:

- 1 cup (packed) light brown sugar
- 1/2 cup light corn syrup
- 3 tablespoons unsalted butter
- 1 1/2 teaspoon salt
- 1/2 cup heavy (whipping) cream
- 1 tablespoon Irish whiskey

1. In a medium saucepan, bring the brown sugar, corn syrup, butter, and salt to a boil over medium heat, whisking to dissolve the sugar. Boil for about 3 minutes or until the mixture is thick and syrupy. Remove from heat.

2. Stir in cream and whiskey until smooth.

3. Serve warm or cool; cover and refrigerate until serving time. Reheat before serving.

Bhofack2 | Dreamstime

STICKY TOFFEE PUDDING
Makes 12 Puddings

THIS deliciously gooey sponge pudding, also known as Sticky Date Pudding in some parts of the globe, is as classic as it gets when it comes to Irish sweets. With origins in British cooking, the recipe continually evolves—some cooks add Guinness; others add nuts—except for the rich toffee sauce that always tops it. You'll find it on menus from the five-star Merrion Hotel in Dublin to the legendary Durty Nelly's Pub in Bunratty, County Clare. At Mikey Ryan's, a gastropub in Cashel, County Tipperary, where this recipe originated, the chef adds a bonus piece of honeycomb and a scoop of vanilla ice cream.

For the Pudding:
- 1 1/2 cups pitted dates
- 1 teaspoon vanilla extract
- 2/3 cup boiling water
- 6 tablespoons butter, at room temperature
- 1/2 cup (packed) light brown sugar
- 2 large eggs
- 2 tablespoons black treacle
- 1 1/2 cups flour
- 1/2 teaspoon baking powder
- 1 1/2 teaspoons baking soda
- Pinch of salt
- 1/2 cup milk

1. Preheat the oven to 325°F. Coat the cups of a standard muffin pan with no-stick baking spray with flour.
2. In a large bowl, soak the dates and vanilla extract in the water for 30 minutes.
3. In the bowl of a stand mixer fitted with a paddle attachment (or with a hand mixer), beat the butter and sugar on medium speed for 2 to 3 minutes or until soft and pale.
4. Beat in the eggs and treacle.
5. Transfer the date mixture to a food processor; process until smooth.
6. Fold into the butter mixture.
7. Sift the flour, baking powder, soda, and salt into the date mixture.
8. Fold in the milk.
9. Spoon the mixture into the prepared pan.
10. Bake for 15 minutes. Rotate pan; bake for another 7 minutes or until a skewer inserted into the center of one comes out clean.
11. Let cool on wire rack for 10 minutes before removing the puddings.

For the Sauce:
- 1 cup sugar
- 4 tablespoons butter, cut into small pieces
- 3/4 cup heavy (whipping) cream

1. In a medium saucepan, slowly heat the sugar over medium heat until it melts and browns.
2. Add the butter a few pieces at a time; whisk until combined.
3. Slowly add the cream; whisk until smooth.

HONEYCOMB
Serves 8 to 10

- 2 cups sugar
- 1/2 cup Lyle's Golden Syrup
- 1/3 cup water
- 1 tablespoon baking soda
- Vanilla ice cream, for serving

1. Line a 9-inch square baking pan with parchment paper, leaving a 2-inch overhang on two sides (to use as handles to lift honeycomb from pan).
2. In a large saucepan, combine the sugar, syrup, and water. Cook over medium-low heat, stirring frequently, until the sugar melts. Continue to cook, without stirring, until the mixture begins to bubble up, turns golden, and registers 300°F on a candy thermometer; remove from the heat.
3. Whisk in the baking soda. (The mixture will bubble up; be careful).
4. Quickly pour the mixture onto the prepared pan; do not spread (this will deflate the bubbles).
5. Leave for at least 2 hours or until the mixture hardens; break it into pieces. To serve, pour a little of the sauce over each pudding; top with a piece of honeycomb. (Store remaining honeycomb in an airtight tin for up to 5 days).

Mikey Ryan's Pub

Monkey Business Images / Dreamstime

SUMMER PUDDING

Serves 6

As its name indicates, summer fruits like strawberries, raspberries, blackberries, and blueberries are the main ingredients in this stunning dessert. But don't be fooled by the word "pudding" in its name, since the other ingredient is white bread or brioche! I was surprised when I discovered it, probably sometime in the early 1990s, although its history dates to the early twentieth century. After the fruit and bread mingle overnight, the result is a colorful dessert that almost looks too pretty to eat. Serve the pudding with whipped or clotted cream.

- 5 cups mixed berries, such as blueberries, strawberries, and raspberries
- 1/2 cup sugar
- 7 slices firm white bread or brioche, crusts removed
- Whipped cream or clotted cream, for serving
- Fresh berries, for garnish (optional)

1. In a medium saucepan, combine the berries and sugar. Cook over medium heat for about 5 minutes or until the berries soften and the sugar dissolves. Remove from heat.

2. Let cool for 10 minutes. Strain the berry mixture, reserving all the juice.

3. Line a 1-quart soufflé dish or mixing bowl with plastic wrap, leaving a 2-inch overhang on both sides to cover the pudding. Cut one piece of bread to fit the bottom of the bowl. Line the sides of the dish with four slices, overlapping each slightly to fill in any gaps. Drizzle some of the juices over the bread.

4. Spoon the berries into the bread-lined bowl. Cover the fruit with the remaining slices, cutting to fit. Drizzle the remaining juice over the top. Cover the pudding with the excess plastic wrap.

5. Lay a plate on top with a weight (like a can of coffee or beans) to ensure that the bread absorbs all the juices; refrigerate overnight.

6. To unmold, remove the weight and plate. Unfold the plastic wrap from the top of the pudding. Place a clean plate on top; quickly invert the pudding. Remove the plastic wrap from the rest of the pudding.

7. To serve, cut the pudding into wedges; top with whipped cream or clotted cream. Garnish with fresh berries, if desired.

STICKY PEAR & GINGER CAKE

Serves 8

The combination of pears and ginger is one that never goes out of fashion. This cake, which is a cross between a *tarte tatin* and a ginger cake, is a perennial favorite in autumn when pears are in season in Ireland and elsewhere. If you're lucky, you might find it on the menu at the Winding Stair, one of Dublin's most beautifully located restaurants overlooking the iconic Ha'Penny Bridge. Serve the cake with a dollop of crème fraîche for just the right balance of sweetness and tang.

For the Cake:

- 1/2 cup granulated sugar
- 1/2 cup packed light brown sugar
- 1 1/2 cups self-rising flour
- 1 tablespoon cinnamon
- 2 tablespoon ground ginger
- 2 teaspoon baking powder
- 2/3 cup canola oil
- 3 large eggs
- 3 pears, peeled and cored
- Crème fraîche, for serving

1. Preheat the oven to 350°F. Coat a 9-inch springform pan with butter flavor no-stick baking spray; top with a round of parchment paper.
2. In a large bowl, whisk together the sugars, flour, cinnamon, ginger, and baking powder.
3. In a small bowl, whisk together the oil and eggs; fold into the flour mixture.
4. Grate two of the pears into the mixture; cut the other pear into slices. Arrange the pear slices, overlapping slightly, on the bottom of the prepared pan; pour the mixture over the pears.
5. Bake the cake for about 45 minutes or until a skewer inserted into the center comes out clean.
6. Let the cake cool on a wire rack for 15 minutes. Remove the side of the pan. Invert the cake onto a large plate. Remove the pan base and parchment paper.

For the Sauce:

- 1/4 cup Lyle's Golden Syrup or light corn syrup
- 1 cup sugar
- 2 tablespoons water
- 2 tablespoons butter
- 1/2 cup heavy (whipping) cream
- 2 teaspoons ground ginger

1. In a medium saucepan, combine the syrup, sugar, and water. Cook over medium heat for 4 to 5 minutes or until the sugar dissolves.

2. Stir in the butter. Add the cream and ground ginger; cook until the sauce is thick and smooth.

3. To serve, cut the cake into slices; spoon the sauce on top. Serve with crème fraîche, if you wish.

Manyakotic / Dreamstime

BUFFALO RICOTTA & BERRY TART

Serves 4 to 6

Dorothy O'Touma provides tours of Macroom Buffalo Farm in County Cork, where farmer Johnny Lynch and his staff transform the milk from his herd of water buffaloes into several types of cheese (see page 32). They make ricotta, an Italian cheese made from water buffalo milk whey, a by-product of the production of other cheeses, and Dorothy creates recipes featuring them. This ricotta tart is a delicious example and one that you can enjoy as a traditional cheesecake or as a single-serve parfait-like dessert. For the parfait version, press the crumbs into the bottom of stem glasses and pipe or spoon the filling on top; drizzle the sauce over the filling.

For the Berry Sauce:

- 6 ounces mixed red berries, frozen or fresh
- 2 tablespoons confectioners' sugar
- Juice of 1/2 lemon

1. In a medium saucepan, cook the berries over medium heat for 8 to 10 minutes or until they begin to soften. (If using fresh berries, add 1 tablespoon water.)
2. Stir in the sugar and lemon juice; mix well.
3. Pass the berries through a fine sieve over a bowl to remove the seeds. Refrigerate.

For the Base:

- 8 to 10 digestive biscuits or shortbread cookies, crushed
- 3 tablespoons butter, melted

1. In a small bowl, combine the crushed biscuits or cookies with the butter.
2. Press into the bottom of a 7-inch springform pan.
3. Refrigerate for at least 15 minutes or until set.

For the Filling:

- 3 ounces cream cheese, at room temperature
- 3/4 cup heavy (whipping) cream
- 2 tablespoons confectioners' sugar
- 1 teaspoon vanilla extract
- 7 ounces ricotta cheese
- Juice of 1/2 lemon

1. In a medium bowl, beat the cream cheese, cream, sugar, and vanilla with an electric mixer on medium speed until stiff peaks form.
2. Fold in the ricotta and lemon juice until smooth.
3. Transfer to the prepared pan; smooth the top. Drizzle the sauce over the top.
4. With a toothpick or wooden skewer, swirl the sauce decoratively through the cake (alternately, spoon the sauce over the slices at serving time).
5. Cover and refrigerate for 4 hours or overnight. To serve, cut the cheesecake into slices.

Antonio Munõz Palomares / Dreamstime

COFFEE & WALNUT CAKE

Serves 10

This Anglo-Irish "gateau," as some like to call it, is a classic cake that ranks—along with Victoria sponge, lemon drizzle, and tea brack—among the most popular teatime cakes in Ireland and the United Kingdom. It frequently appears at teatime on tea trays and cake trolleys in Irish country house hotels and is a long-standing favorite with cooks hosting tea at home.

For the Cake:

- 2 teaspoons instant espresso granules or powder
- 1/4 cup warm water
- 16 tablespoons butter, at room temperature
- 1 cup sugar
- 4 large eggs
- 2 cups self-rising flour
- 1 1/3 cup chopped walnuts, plus more for decorating
- 8 to 12 walnut halves, for decorating

For the Icing:

- 10 tablespoons unsalted butter, at room temperature
- Pinch of salt
- 4 1/2 cups confectioners' sugar
- 4 tablespoons brewed espresso

1. Preheat the oven to 350°F. Coat the bottom and sides of two 8-inch cake pans with no-stick baking spray with flour.

2. In a small bowl, mix the espresso granules with the water; stir to dissolve.

3. In a stand mixer fitted with a paddle attachment (or with a hand mixer), beat the butter and sugar on medium speed until light and fluffy.

4. Add the eggs, one at a time, alternating with the flour. Beat until blended and smooth.

5. Stir in the nuts and espresso.

6. Divide the mixture into the prepared pans.

7. Bake the cakes for 28 to 30 minutes or until a skewer inserted into the center comes out clean. Let the cakes cool in the pans for 10 minutes. Invert cakes onto a wire rack; return to upright.

8. Make the icing. In a stand mixer fitted with a paddle attachment (or with a hand mixer), beat the butter, salt, confectioners' sugar, and espresso until smooth.

9. Brush any loose crumbs from the cake layers. Place one layer, rounded side down, on a serving plate.

10. With an offset spatula, spread 1/3 to 1/2 cup of the icing over the first layer to within about 1/4 inch of the edge. Place the second cake layer, rounded side up, on top. Coat the side of the cake with a thin layer of icing.

11. Refrigerate the cake for 20 minutes.

12. Spread the remaining icing on top and around the side. Press remaining chopped walnuts on side. Decoratively place the walnut halves around the top of the cake.

Boris Ryzhov / Dreamstime

FALLEN CHOCOLATE CAKE WITH BROWN BREAD ICE CREAM

Serves 8 to 10

CHOCOLATE lovers rejoice at making and eating rich, flourless chocolate cake. I've enjoyed it in Ireland over the years topped with a simple dollop of freshly whipped cream, warm fruit compote, and, lately, with Dingle-made Murphy's Brown Bread Ice Cream. Specializing in ice cream made with milk from the rare, indigenous breed of Kerry cow, free range eggs, organic sugar, and even their own sea salt from Dingle, the Murphy family thinks theirs is the best you'll ever taste! If you can't visit any of the places in Ireland where their ice cream shops are located—Dingle, Dublin, Killarney, Galway, or Kildare—try this recipe inspired by the famous ice cream maker for a taste of Ireland at home. In addition to being a perfect topping for this chocolate cake, brown bread ice cream is also a great way to use up leftover bread (see pages 27, 28, and 29); alternately, use store-bought bread, such as the John McCambridge brand.[1] Make the ice cream a day ahead of serving, preferably in an ice cream maker.

For the Ice Cream:

- 5 to 6 slices stale brown soda bread
- 1/2 cup packed dark brown sugar
- 1 cup milk
- 3/4 cup sugar
- Pinch of salt
- 2 cups heavy cream
- 1 tablespoon vanilla bean paste

1. Preheat the oven to 350°F. Line a baking sheet with aluminum foil.
2. Crumble the bread slices into small pieces to measure 2 cups. In a medium bowl, toss with sugar. Spread the crumb mixture out on the prepared baking sheet.
3. Bake, stirring occasionally to prevent sticking, for 20 to 25 minutes or until the crumbs are crisp and caramelized. Let cool.
4. With a hand mixer on low speed, beat the milk, sugar, and salt just until the sugar is dissolved.
5. Stir in the heavy cream and vanilla.
6. Cover; refrigerate for about 2 hours, preferably overnight.
7. Spoon the mixture into a frozen freezer bowl of an ice cream maker (such as Cuisinart); process according to the manufacturer's directions until the mixture thickens.

---

[1] You can order the McCambridge brand of brown bread online at *www.foodireland.com*

8. Once churned, add the brown breadcrumbs; process for 5 minutes longer.
9. Transfer the ice cream to an airtight container; freeze until firm and ready to serve. (Remove from freezer about 10 minutes before serving).

For the Cake:

- 8 tablespoons butter, at room temperature
- 1 cup sugar
- 6 large eggs, separated
- 6 ounces bittersweet (not unsweetened) chocolate, melted and cooled
- 1 teaspoon vanilla extract
- 1 1/2 cup ground almonds
- 1/4 teaspoon salt

1. Preheat the oven to 350° F. Coat a 9-inch springform pan with no-stick baking spray with flour.
2. In a stand mixer fitted with the paddle attachment (or with a hand mixer), beat the butter and 3/4 cup of the sugar on medium speed for 2 to 3 minutes or until pale and fluffy.
3. Beat in the egg yolks, one at a time.
4. Beat in the chocolate and vanilla.
5. Beat in the almonds and salt.
6. In a stand mixer fitted with the whisk attachment (or with a hand mixer), beat the egg whites on medium-low speed until soft peaks form.
7. Gradually add the remaining 1/4 cup of sugar. Beat until stiff peaks form.
8. Spoon one quarter of the egg whites into the chocolate mixture to lighten; gently fold in the remaining whites until combined.
9. Transfer the mixture to the prepared pan; smooth the top.
10. Bake the cake for 30 to 40 minutes or until the top is firm. (Cake will rise, form a crust, then fall again.)
11. Cool completely. Run a knife around the inside of the pan; remove the side.
12. To serve, cut the cake into slices; serve with the ice cream.

Teresa Verbickis / Dreamstime

IRISH APPLE CAKE

Serves 6

APPLES have been grown in Ireland for three thousand years. Eating apples, cooking apples, and cider apples are all grown there, with Bramley's Seedling (Bramley for short) the variety most widely planted in places from County Armagh to Tipperary and Waterford. You'll find this apple, known as an outstanding "cooker" because of its high acid content and stiff but light texture, used in this old-fashioned apple cake, one of the most popular sweets in Irish cookery. A good substitute for the Bramley is Granny Smith, Winesap, Fuji, or Honeycrisp. Serve the cake with vanilla ice cream, whipped cream, or clotted cream.

- 8 tablespoons butter, at room temperature
- 1/2 cup sugar
- 2 eggs
- 2 tablespoons milk
- 2 cups self-rising flour
- 3 cooking apples, peeled and thinly sliced
- 1 tablespoon brown sugar
- 2 tablespoons sliced almonds

1. Preheat the oven to 350°F. Line a 9-inch round baking pan with parchment paper; lightly coat the paper with no-stick baking spray with flour.
2. In a stand mixer fitted with a paddle attachment (or with a hand mixer), beat the butter and sugar on medium speed until light and fluffy.
3. Beat in the eggs and milk.
4. Fold in the flour; fold in the apples.
5. Transfer the mixture to the prepared pan; smooth the top. Sprinkle with brown sugar and almonds.
6. Bake the cake for 40 to 45 minutes or until the top is brown and a skewer inserted into the center comes out clean.
7. Let cool on a wire rack for about 15 minutes before cutting into slices.
8. Serve warm with some whipped cream or vanilla ice cream.

BLOOD ORANGE & POLENTA CAKES

Makes 8 mini loaves

The almond-polenta mix in these little cakes seems like a perfect combination; add blood orange juice and orange blossom water to it to seal the deal! Inspired by a recipe from Dooks Fine Foods in Fethard, County Tipperary (pictured opposite), orange blossom water, which is made from the petals of the bitter orange tree, provides a flowery and fruity aroma that perfumes the loaves. Drizzle with orange glaze and a slice of blood orange for a pretty-as-a-picture dessert.

For the Cakes:

- 12 tablespoons unsalted butter, at room temperature
- 3/4 cup sugar
- 1 1/2 cups fine almond flour
- 3/4 cup fine polenta
- 1 1/2 teaspoons baking powder
- 1/4 teaspoon salt
- 3 large eggs
- 1/2 teaspoon orange water
- 1/3 cup blood orange juice
- 1 tablespoon blood orange zest
- Blood orange slices, for garnish (optional)

1. Preheat the oven to 350°F. Coat eight 4x2 1/2-inch mini loaf pans with no-stick baking spray with flour.
2. In the bowl of a stand mixer fitted with a paddle attachment (or with a hand mixer), beat the butter and sugar on medium speed until light and fluffy.
3. In a medium bowl, whisk together the almond flour, polenta, baking powder, and salt.

Margaret M. Johnson

For the Cakes (Cont.)

4. Beat 3 to 4 tablespoons of the flour mixture into the butter mixture.
5. Beat in the eggs, one at a time, alternating with the remaining flour mixture.
6. Stir in the orange water, juice, and zest.
7. Spoon the mixture into the prepared pans, filling each about 3/4 full.
8. Bake the cakes for 25 to 28 minutes or until a skewer inserted into the center of one cake comes out clean.
9. Let the cakes cool on a wire rack for 20 minutes. Run a knife around the edge of the pans. Invert cakes onto the rack; let cool completely.

For the Icing:

- 1 cup confectioners' sugar
- 2 tablespoons blood orange juice, plus more if needed
- 1 1/2 teaspoons orange water

1. In a small bowl, whisk together the confectioners' sugar, orange juice, and orange water until smooth (adjust consistency with additional orange juice).
2. Drizzle the icing over the cake; top with an orange slice, if desired.

LEMON LOAF WITH ROSEMARY DRIZZLE

Makes 1 loaf

It's safe to say that you'll find slices of this classic cake offered in tea rooms, coffee shops, home kitchens, and take-aways throughout the Emerald Isle. It's a "standard" to which bakers often add a personal touch: think extra lemon (or orange) zest in the cake or fresh herbs in the drizzle. The folks at Nicholas Mosse (Bennettsbridge, County Kilkenny), one of Ireland's most well-known pottery brands, favor the cake so much that they suggest you add fresh rosemary to the topping and serve it (pictured opposite) on one of the pieces in its Wildflower Collection: Clematis, Blue Blossom, and Wildflower Meadow.

For the Cake:

- 10 tablespoons butter
- 1 1/2 cups demerara sugar
- 2 large eggs
- Zest of 1 lemon
- 1/2 cup milk
- 1/4 teaspoon salt
- 1 1/2 cups self-rising flour, sifted

1. Preheat the oven to 350°F. Coat a 9-inch loaf pan with no-stick baking spray. Line the pan with parchment paper, leaving a 2-inch overhang on both sides (to use as handles to lift the cake from the pan).
2. In a stand mixer fitted with a paddle (or with a hand mixer), beat the butter and sugar on medium speed until light and fluffy.
3. Beat in the eggs and zest.
4. Beat in the milk, salt, and flour until the mixture is smooth.
5. Transfer to the prepared pan; smooth the top.
6. Bake the cake for about 45 minutes or until the top is brown and a skewer inserted into the center comes out clean.
7. Let cool on a wire rack for about 5 minutes; lift the cake from the pan. Prick the top with a fork.

For the Drizzle:

- 6 tablespoons water
- 2 tablespoons sugar
- Juice of 1 lemon
- 4 sprigs fresh rosemary

1. In a small saucepan, bring the water, sugar, lemon juice, and rosemary to a boil. Cook for about 2 minutes or until the sugar dissolves.
2. Reduce heat; simmer for 5 minutes.
3. Let steep for 10 minutes; strain the rosemary.
4. Slowly drizzle the warm syrup over the cake.
5. Let cool completely before cutting into slices. (The cake is best eaten fresh but will keep in an airtight container in the refrigerator for a week or wrap and freeze for up to 3 months).

Nicholas Mosse Pottery, Kilkenny

Helen Schofield / Dreamstime

LEMON POSSET WITH BLUEBERRY COMPOTE

Serves 4

A posset is an old-fashioned drink originally made with hot milk and flavored with spices. It was once drunk as a delicacy and even as a remedy for colds. More recently, the drink has become popular as a refreshing, oh-so-simple dessert and is particularly appealing served in a stemmed or decorative glass and topped with blueberry compote or a few fresh berries. Serve the posset with shortbread "fingers" (page 122).

For the Posset:

- 2 1/2 cups heavy (whipping) cream
- 1/2 cup sugar
- Zest and juice of 3 lemons

1. In a medium saucepan, bring the cream and sugar to a boil.
2. Reduce heat. Simmer, stirring constantly, for about 5 minutes or until smooth.
3. Stir in the juice and zest.
4. Remove from the heat; let cool for 10 minutes.
5. Pour into stemmed or decorative glasses; refrigerate for 12 hours or until set.

For the Compote:

- 2 cups fresh blueberries
- 3 tablespoons water
- 1/4 cup sugar
- 2 teaspoons fresh lemon juice

1. In a medium saucepan, combine 1 cup of blueberries, water, sugar, and lemon juice; cook over medium heat for about 10 minutes.
2. Add the remaining blueberries; cook, stirring frequently, for 5 to 6 minutes longer.
3. Remove from heat; let cool completely.
4. To serve, spoon the compote over the posset.

PEAR, APRICOT, & ALMOND ROULADE
Serves 6

RENVYLE House is a historic country house hotel located along the shores of the Wild Atlantic Way in Connemara, County Galway. Over several centuries, it has been built, pulled down, rebuilt, burned to ashes, and rebuilt again. It was once the home of a powerful Gaelic chieftain and, in more modern times, the home of Irish poet, statesman, and surgeon Oliver St. John Gogarty. Since becoming a country house hotel in 1883, Renvyle has played host to many famous people, including writer/playwright Lady Augusta Gregory, poet/politician William Butler Yeats, and Prime Minister Winston Churchill, to name a few. The house, under the direction of the Coyle family since 1952, has its own lake, private beach, stunning gardens, and award-winning Rusheeduff, the restaurant that inspired this yummy roulade.

- 4 ounces dried apricots, chopped
- 2 tablespoons honey
- 1 tablespoon fresh lemon juice
- 1/2 cup packed light brown sugar
- 2 Anjou or Bartlett pears, peeled, cored, and diced
- 1/4 cup ground almonds
- 2 tablespoons sliced almonds
- 1 sheet frozen puff pastry, thawed
- 1 egg mixed with 1 tablespoon water, for egg wash
- Confectioners' sugar, for dusting
- Vanilla ice cream, for serving

1. Preheat the oven to 375°F. Line a baking sheet with parchment paper.
2. In a small saucepan, combine the apricots, honey, lemon juice, brown sugar, and pears. Cook over medium heat for about 5 minutes or until the apricots begin to soften.
3. Remove from heat; let cool.
4. Stir in the almonds.
5. Sprinkle a work surface with flour. Unroll the pastry sheet; roll into a 14x11-inch rectangle. With the long side facing you, spoon the fruit mixture onto the lower third of the pastry. Starting at the long side, roll up like a jelly roll. Tuck the ends under to seal.
6. Place the pastry seamside down on the prepared baking pan; brush with egg wash. Cut several 2-inch-long slits 2 inches apart on the top.
7. Bake the roulade for 25 minutes or until puffed and golden.
8. Cool on the baking sheet on a wire rack for 15 minutes; dust with confectioners' sugar.
9. To serve, cut the roulade into slices; serve with ice cream.

PROFITEROLES WITH CHOCOLATE SAUCE

Makes about 20 profiteroles

Profiteroles, also known as cream puffs, are dreamy, little sweets made with choux pastry and filled with crème pâtissière, ice cream, or whipped cream, as in this recipe. I think of them as quite an old-fashioned dessert, but they still appear on restaurant menus (like the ones pictured opposite from Kilkea Castle in County Kildare) and in homes, where they make for a perfect ending to an elegant meal. The rich, fudgy chocolate sauce drizzled on top is nearly obligatory, although a simple dusting of confectioners' sugar works, too!

For the Profiteroles:

- 1 cup water
- 8 tablespoons unsalted butter
- 1 teaspoon sugar
- 1/4 teaspoon salt
- 1 cup flour
- 4 large eggs
- Crème pâtissière or whipped cream, for filling

1. Preheat the oven to 400°F. Line 2 baking sheets with parchment paper.
2. In a medium saucepan, bring the butter, sugar, and salt to a boil.
3. Add the flour all at once, stirring vigorously with a wooden spoon until the mixture forms a ball and pulls away from the side of the pan. Remove from heat.
4. Add the eggs, one at a time, beating well after each addition.
5. Return the pan to medium-low heat; continue to beat for about 2 minutes or until nearly smooth.
6. Spoon the batter into a large pastry bag fitted with a 1/2-inch plain tip. Pipe about 10 balls onto each prepared pan, spacing them about 1 1/2 inches apart, or drop the batter by rounded teaspoons onto the pans. With a wet finger, lightly press down the swirl at the top of each puff.
7. Bake for 30 to 35 minutes, rotating the baking sheets between upper and lower racks halfway through baking or until puffed and golden.
8. Transfer to a wire rack to cool completely.

For the Sauce:

- 8 ounces semi-sweet chocolate (chips or chunks)
- 1 1/2 cups heavy (whipping) cream

1. Place the chips or chunks and cream in a microwave-safe bowl or measuring cup. Heat over low heat or in the microwave until the cream is very hot.

2. Remove from the heat; stir until the chocolate is melted and smooth. Keep warm.

3. To serve, cut each profiterole in half horizontally with a serrated knife. (Remove and discard any moist dough inside).

4. Spoon or pipe about 1 rounded tablespoon of crème pâtissière or whipped cream into the bottom of each and replace the top.

5. Arrange on dessert plates and drizzle with chocolate sauce.

Margaret M. Johnson

Anna Denisova / Dreamstime

RHUBARB & ELDERFLOWER CRUMBLE
Makes 6

For a brief period in spring, the rush to rhubarb is frenetic with crisps, cakes, pies, tarts, jams, and chutneys serving as a few of the ways this colorful vegetable makes its way into Irish cookery. The recipe for this crumble, a recent discovery at an Avoca café in Wicklow, lets the rhubarb stand on its own with only a little sweetening from elderflower cordial, a lovely contemporary touch. Both the crumble and filling are made separately and can be assembled and reheated at serving time. Serve the crumbles in individual ramekins topped with whipped cream or vanilla ice cream.

For the Crumble:

- 2 cups flour
- 16 tablespoons butter, cut into small pieces
- 3/4 cup packed light brown sugar
- 1 cup Irish oatmeal
- 1/2 cup chopped hazelnuts
- 1 1/4 cups flaked almonds

1. Preheat the oven to 325°F. Line a baking sheet with parchment paper.
2. In a large bowl, combine the flour, butter, brown sugar, oatmeal, hazelnuts, and almonds. With your fingertips, rub the mixture together to form small clusters. Spread out on the prepared pan.
3. Bake, stirring every 5 minutes, for 35 to 40 minutes or until browned and crisp.

For the Rhubarb:

- 1 1/2 pounds rhubarb, cut into 1-inch pieces
- 3/4 cup sugar
- 1 teaspoon vanilla extract
- 2 tablespoons elderflower cordial
- Zest of 1/2 lemon
- Whipped cream or vanilla ice cream, for serving

1. In a medium saucepan, combine the rhubarb, sugar, vanilla, elderflower cordial, and lemon zest. Cook over medium heat, stirring once or twice, for 5 to 7 minutes or until the rhubarb is nearly tender. (Do not overcook.)
2. To serve, spoon the fruit into six 4-ounce ramekins; top with the crumble (freeze leftover crumble in resealable plastic bags). Serve with whipped cream or vanilla ice cream, if desired. (To make ahead, assemble fruit and crumble. Reheat in a 325°F oven for 10 to 15 minutes).

SHORTBREAD

Makes 14 fingers

SHORTBREAD may have been a Scottish "invention" (food historians often credit the cooks at Scottish Queen Mary's court with introducing it), but its popularity spread quickly to other parts of the empire and, eventually, to Ireland. The buttery biscuits can be shaped into squares, rounds, or "fingers"; they keep well in an airtight tin for at least two weeks.

- 16 tablespoons unsalted butter, room temperature
- 3/4 cup confectioners' sugar
- 1 teaspoon vanilla extract
- 2 cups flour
- 1/4 teaspoon salt

1. Coat a 14x4-inch rectangular tart pan with a removable bottom with no-stick baking spray.
2. In a large bowl, beat butter with an electric mixer on medium speed for 3 to 4 minutes or until smooth.
3. Gradually beat in sugar and vanilla extract. In a small bowl, whisk together flour and salt; gradually beat into the butter mixture until smooth.
4. Pat and spread the dough into the prepared pan. With a fork, prick in several places to prevent the dough from rising. Refrigerate for 30 minutes.
5. Preheat the oven to 300°F. Bake the shortbread for 55 to 60 minutes or until the top is pale and the edge is golden.
6. Let cool on a wire rack for 10 to 15 minutes. Lift out the bottom of the pan; cut the shortbread into 14 fingers.

Monkey Business Images / Dreamstime

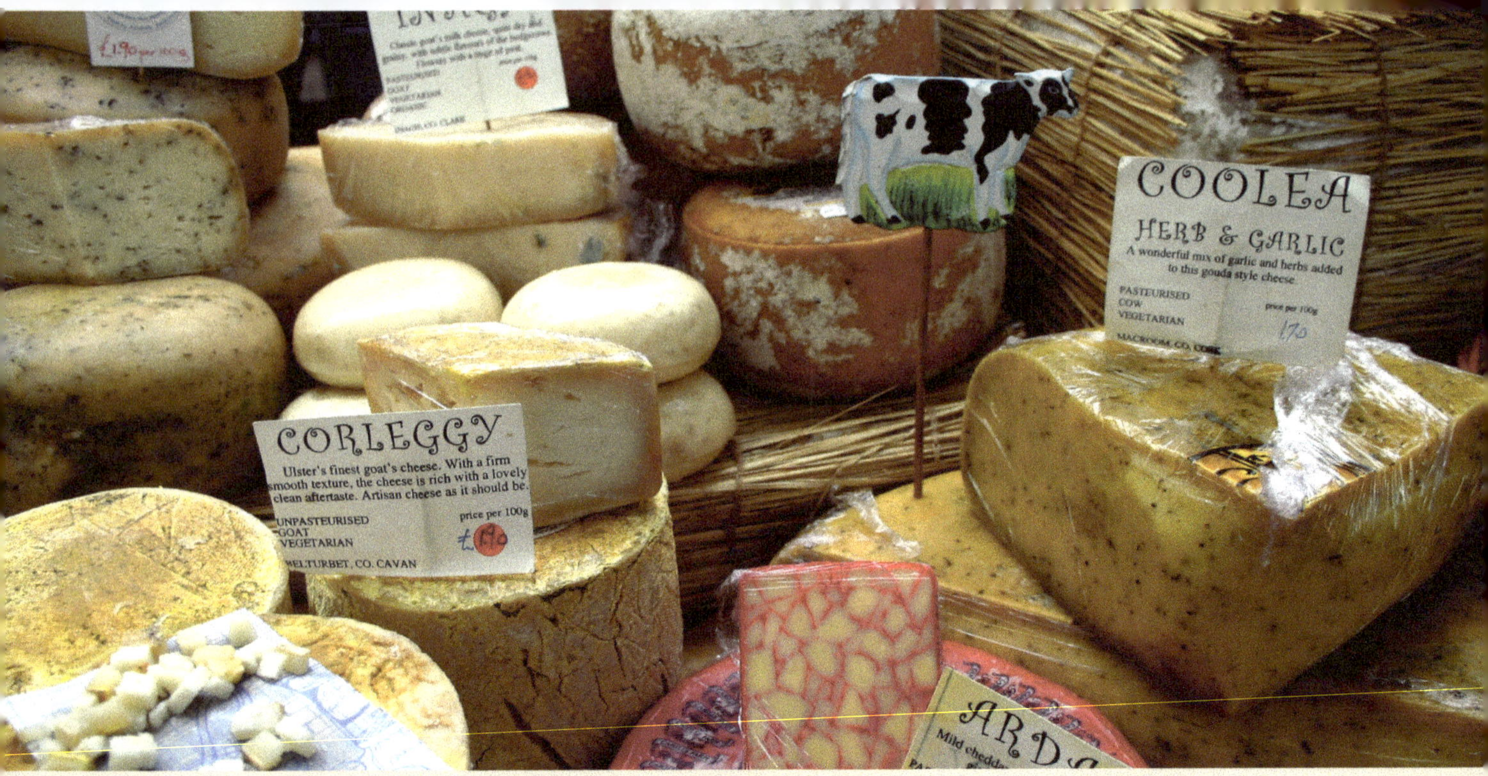
CORLEGGY
Ulster's finest goat's cheese. With a firm smooth texture, the cheese is rich with a lovely clean aftertaste. Artisan cheese as it should be.
UNPASTEURISED
GOAT
VEGETARIAN
price per 100g
BELTURBET, CO. CAVAN
COOLEA
HERB & GARLIC
A wonderful mix of garlic and herbs added to this gouda style cheese.
PASTEURISED
COW
VEGETARIAN
price per 100g
MACROOM, CO. CORK

Gubbeen Farmhouse Products
Schull, Co Cork, Ireland

YOUNG BUCK

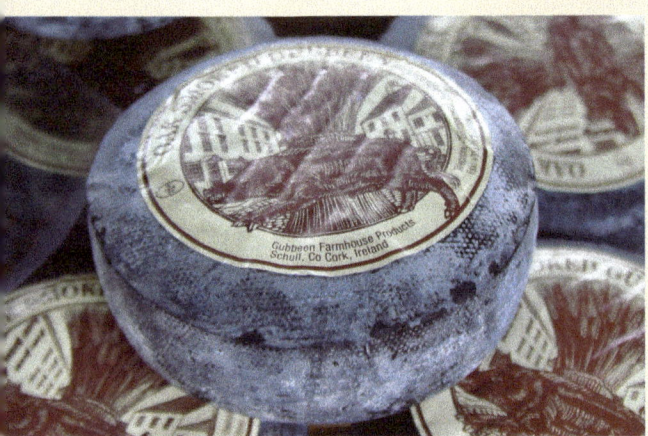

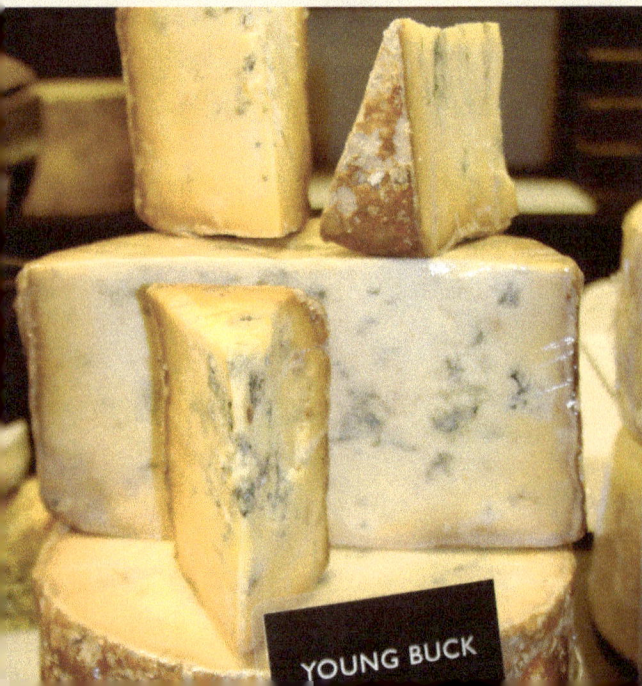

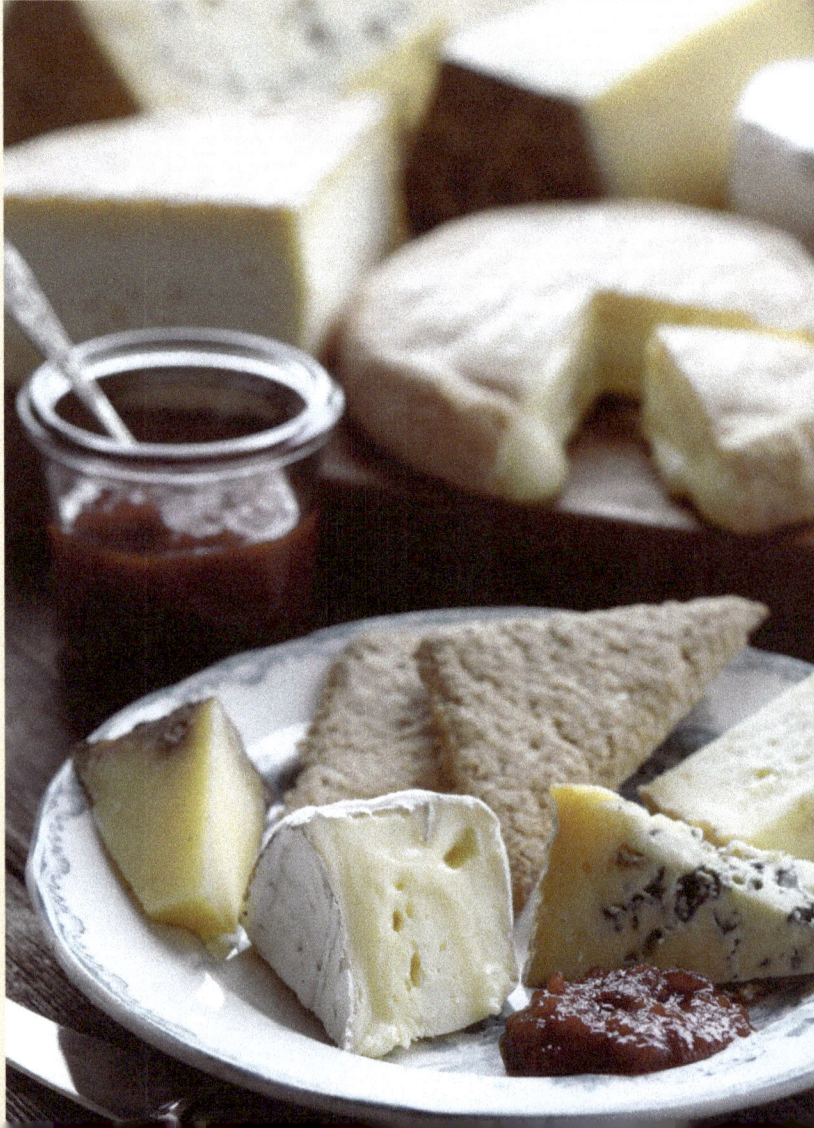

THE CHEESE COURSE

*Cheese making forms a central part of any culture.
You only have to look at the paintings of the Renaissance,
which always had a great big wheel of crumbling cheese in among the figs
and pomegranates to know that cheese is a staff of civilization as well as life.*
—Helene Willems, Founder, Coolea Farmhouse Cheese

Dairy products have always been important in the Irish diet—from the rich cream and butter added to potato dishes like Colcannon and Champ to the buttermilk that's mixed with baking soda as a leavening agent in brown bread. Irish people probably drink more milk than most other people in the world, and cream-laden puddings are an integral part of many Irish meals. Cheese, however, is another story, at least until the late 1970s when artisan cheese-making began in earnest with a few enterprising dairy farmers launching a natural revival of the age-old craft. The first cheeses were made to satisfy the desire for more interesting food than was currently available; later ones were developed by European expats, who had moved to Ireland and missed their native cheeses.

Writing in "Bon Appétit" magazine in 1996, Irish food writer Clare Boylan called what was going on then, especially in County Cork, "a quiet revolution";[1] and by 1983, the number of trailblazer farmers successfully producing a range of cheeses grew enough to form CÁIS, the Association of Irish Farmhouse Cheesemakers. Membership now numbers nearly forty producers of cow, goat, sheep, and buffalo milk cheeses, with many other producers working away to bring outstanding artisan cheeses to Irish tables.

Slowly but surely, Irish farmhouse cheeses grew in popularity and demand. Brothers Kevin and Seamus Sheridan started selling a small selection of native cheeses at their stall at the Galway farmers' market, and in 1995, they opened a full-fledged cheese shop a few steps away on Church Yard Street with Irish farmhouse cheeses piled from floor to ceiling. Later that year, they opened a shop on South Anne Street in Dublin, where Irish cheeses were quickly joined by their European cousins. Today, Sheridans Cheesemongers includes maturing rooms in County Meath and twenty-one locations (independent shops and counters in Dunnes Stores) from Waterford to Tralee offering artisan cheese, food, and wine.

---

1 Clare Boylan, "For the Love of Cheese," *Bon Appétit*, May 1996, 42.

Opposite page (clockwise, from top): ST. GEORGE'S MARKET, Belfast, Margaret M. Johnson; CHEESE BOARD WITH CHUTNEY, Bord Bia (Irish Food Board); YOUNG BUCK CHEESE, Belfast, Margaret M. Johnson; GUBBEEN CHEESE, Schull, Co. Cork, Margaret M. Johnson

Monkey Business Images / Dreamstime

Beyond a nibble here and there, it was only a matter of time for the Irish to embrace the cheese course—that beloved French tradition of serving cheese after a meal in place of or in addition to dessert. Frequently quoted French gastronome Jean Anthelme Brillat-Savarin admired the post-prandial tradition so much that in 1825, he wrote, "Dessert without cheese is like a beauty with only one eye." A selection of Irish cheeses offered after dinner, sometimes even a "cheese trolley," has become the new "fourth course" on most Irish restaurant menus as well as at meals at home.

Served with biscuits or crackers, chutney or fruits, membrillo (quince paste) or honey, cheeses are selected for a variety of taste and texture. Selections will include soft or semi-soft cheeses like Cooleeney or Durrus; semi-firm cheeses like Coolea or Knockanore; blue-veined beauties like Cashel Blue or Wicklow Blue; a goat or sheep cheese like Ardsallagh or St. Tola; and a hard cheese like Coolatin or Hegarty's cheddar. In the U.S., artisan cheese shops stock a number of Irish cheeses; alternately, you can buy some online at igourmet.com and murrayscheese.com. Cheeses from the Kerrygold brand—Dubliner, Cheddar, Swiss, Blarney, Skellig, and Cashel Blue—are widely available in supermarkets. Offer your cheese course with one of these chutneys for a genuine Irish finish to your meal!

THE CHEESE COURSE

Apple & Pear Chutney	129
Cranberry-Walnut Chutney	129
Fig Chutney	130
Fig Jam	130
Rhubarb-orange Chutney	131

Yurii Yarema | Dreamstime

APPLE & PEAR CHUTNEY

Makes 1 1/2 cups

- 1/3 cup chopped onion
- 1/3 cup cider vinegar
- 1 teaspoon minced fresh ginger
- 1 cup packed dark brown sugar
- 3/4 cup golden raisins
- 1 1/2 cups diced apples
- 1 1/2 cups diced pears
- 1/4 cup chopped walnuts (optional)

1. In a large nonreactive saucepan, bring the onion, vinegar, ginger, sugar, raisins, apples, and pears to a boil.
2. Reduce the heat to medium-low. Cook, stirring frequently, for 20 to 25 minutes or until the mixture thickens.
3. Stir in the walnuts (if using).
4. Spoon the hot mixture into clean glass canning jars or plastic freezer containers, leaving at least a half inch of headspace.
5. Refrigerate for up to 4 weeks or freeze. Return to room temperature for serving.

CRANBERRY-WALNUT CHUTNEY

Makes 2 cups

- 1 1/2 cups cranberries
- 2/3 cup packed brown sugar
- 1/2 cup chopped dates
- 1/3 cup chopped celery
- 1/3 cup diced apple
- 1 tablespoon chopped candied ginger
- 1 tablespoon fresh lemon juice
- 1/2 onion, finely chopped
- 1/4 cup water
- 1/4 cup chopped walnuts

1. In a large nonreactive saucepan, combine all the ingredients except the walnuts. Bring to a boil over medium heat.
2. Reduce heat to medium-low. Cook, uncovered, for 15 to 20 minutes or until the mixture thickens.
3. Stir occasionally. Stir in the walnuts.
4. Refrigerate in a covered plastic container for up to 2 weeks. Return to room temperature for serving.

FIG CHUTNEY

Makes about 3 cups

- 1 cup packed light brown sugar
- 1 cup apple cider vinegar
- 2 pounds fresh figs (a combination of Mission and Kadota), stemmed, halved, and cut into bite-sized pieces
- 1 Granny Smith apple, peeled, cored, and chopped
- 1 medium onion, chopped
- 1 cup golden raisins
- 1 1/2 teaspoon sea salt

1. In a large nonreactive saucepan, bring the sugar, vinegar, figs, apple, onion, raisins, and salt to a boil; cook for 3 to 5 minutes.
2. Reduce the heat to low. Cook for 45 to 50 minutes or until the mixture thickens.
3. Spoon the hot mixture into clean glass canning jars or plastic freezer containers, leaving at least a half inch of headspace.
4. Refrigerate for up to 4 weeks or freeze. Return to room temperature for serving.

FIG JAM

Makes 2 cups

- 2 pounds fresh figs (a combination of Mission and Kadota), stemmed, halved, and cut into bite-sized pieces
- 1 3/4 cups sugar
- 1 lemon, seeded and thinly sliced
- 1 cinnamon stick

1. In a large nonreactive saucepan, combine the figs and sugar; stir to distribute sugar. Cover and leave overnight.
2. Over medium-high heat, cook the fig mixture for 4 to 5 minutes or until the sugar dissolves; stir in the lemon and cinnamon stick.
3. Reduce the heat to low. Cook, stirring frequently, for about 2 hours or until the mixture thickens and registers 220°F on a candy thermometer.
4. With kitchen shears, cut the lemon rind into bite-sized pieces. Remove the cinnamon stick.
5. Spoon the hot mixture into clean glass canning jars or plastic freezer containers, leaving at least a half inch of headspace.
6. Refrigerate for up to 4 weeks or freeze. Return to room temperature for serving.

RHUBARB-ORANGE CHUTNEY

Makes 3 cups

- 4 seedless oranges, segmented
- 3 pounds rhubarb, cut into 1-inch pieces
- 3 medium onions, chopped
- 1 cup golden raisins
- 1 cup sultanas
- 3 1/4 cups malt vinegar
- 3 1/3 cups packed light brown sugar
- 1 teaspoon ground mace
- 1 teaspoon ground cinnamon
- 1 teaspoon ground allspice

1. Cut the orange segments into small pieces, reserving the juice.

2. In a large non-reactive saucepan, combine the oranges and juice with the remaining ingredients. Bring to a boil.

3. Reduce the heat to medium-low. Cook, stirring frequently, for about 2 hours or until the mixture thickens.

4. Spoon the hot mixture into clean glass canning jars or plastic freezer containers, leaving at least a half inch of headspace.

5. Refrigerate for up to 4 weeks or freeze. Return to room temperature for serving.

Lidipapp | Dreamstime

DOOLIN, County Clare, *Margaret M. Johnson*

INDEX

A

Apples,
> Apple & Pear Chutney, 129
>
> Celeriac & Apple Remoulade, 45
>
> Irish Apple Cake, 109
>
> Potato, Apple & Parsnip Purée, 80

B

Beetroot,
> Purée, 62
>
> Roasted Beetroot & Citrus Salad with Cashel Blue Cheese, 38

Boxty, 83

Blood Orange & Polenta Cakes, 110

Bread & Butter Pudding with Whiskey & Caramel Sauce, 94

Breads,
> Brown Bread Ice Cream, 106
>
> Guinness & Malt Wheaten Bread, 28
>
> Kinsale Brown Soda Bread, 27
>
> Walnut & Treacle Bread, 29

Buffalo Ricotta & Berry Tart, 102

C

Café Paradiso, 36, 84

Cakes,
> Blood Orange & Polenta, 110
>
> Blue Cheese Potato, 84
>
> Coffee & Walnut, 104

Fallen Chocolate Cake with Brown Bread
    Ice Cream, 106

Irish Apple, 10

Lemon Loaf with
    Rosemary Drizzle, 112

Sticky Pear & Ginger, 100

Cashel Blue,
    Cashel Blue Tartine with Roasted Figs & Prosciutto, 30
    Roasted Beetroot & Citrus Salad with Cashel Blue Cheese, 38

Cauliflower,
    Roasted Cauliflower Steaks, 70
    Cauliflower & Couscous Salad, 71

Celeriac,
    Celeriac & Apple Remoulade, 45
    Celeriac Mash, 79
    Potato & Celeriac Soup, 19

Champ, 77

Cheese,
    Buffalo,
        Macroom Buffalo, 32
        Ricotta & Berry Tart, 102
        Toons Bridge Dairy, 32
    Cashel Blue,
        Blue Cheese Potato Cakes, 84
        Cashel Blue Tartine with Roasted Figs & Prosciutto, 30
        Roasted Beetroot & Citrus Salad with Cashel Blue Cheese, 38
    Course, 125
    Goat,
        Goat Cheese Tarts with Red Onion Marmalade, 34
        Goat Cheese & Tomato Charlottes, 36
        Goat Cheese-stuffed Chicken Wrapped in Prosciutto, 61

    Grilled Halloumi with Courgettes & Mushrooms, 73
    Sheridans Cheesemongers, 125

Chilli-smoked Salmon Fritters, 44

Chimichurri, 53

Chocolate,
    Fallen Chocolate Cake with Brown Bread Ice Cream, 106
    Sauce, 118

Chutney,
    Apple & Pear, 129
    Cranberry-walnut, 129
    Fig, 130
    Rhubarb-orange, 131

Cobh Seafood Pie, 65

Coffee & Walnut Cake, 104

Colcannon, 78

Cranberry-walnut Chutney, 129

D

Dauphinoise Potatoes, 90

F

Fallen Chocolate Cake with Brown Bread Ice Cream, 106

Figs,
    Cashel Blue Tartine with Roasted Figs & Prosciutto, 30
    Chutney, 130
    Jam, 130

Filet of Beef with Irish Whiskey Sauce, 58

G

Goat Cheese-stuffed Chicken Wrapped in Prosciutto, 61

Grilled Halloumi with Courgettes & Mushrooms, 73

Guinness & Malt Wheaten Bread, 28

H

Honeycomb, 97

Hot Smoked Salmon Chowder, 43

I

Irish Apple Cake, 109

Irish Stew, 55

K

Kinsale Brown Soda Bread, 27

L

Lamb,
- Chops with Honey, Apricot & Tarragon Sauce, 54
- Croquettes, 24
- Irish Stew, 55
- Loin of Lamb with Parsley & Mint Sauce, 52
- Shepherd's Pie with Cheddar Crust, 56

Lemon,
- Loaf with Rosemary Drizzle, 112
- Posset with Blueberry Compote, 115

M

Mini Potato Gratins, 88

Mushrooms,
- Garryhinch Wood Exotic Mushrooms, 33
- Grilled Halloumi with Courgettes & Mushrooms, 73
- Warm Mushroom & Black Pudding Salad, 40
- Wild Mushrooms & Ricotta Toast, 33

P

Pan-seared Cod with Seaweed Butter, 66

Pan-seared Duck Breast with Beetroot Purée, 62

Pan-seared Salmon with Dill & Caper Sauce, 68

Pears,
- Apple & Pear Chutney, 129
- Pear, Apricot, & Almond Roulade, 117
- Sticky Pear & Ginger Cake, 100

Potatoes,
- Boxty, 83
- Blue Cheese Potato Cakes, 84
- Celeriac Mash, 79
- Champ, 77
- Colcannon, 78
- Dauphinoise, 90
- Debate, 91
- Mini Potato Gratins, 88
- Potato, Apple, & Parsnip Purée, 80
- Potato & Celeriac Soup, 19
- Three-Cheese Rösti, 86

Profiteroles with Chocolate Sauce, 118

Puddings,
- Black,
  - Clonakilty, 40
  - Warm Mushroom & Black Pudding Salad, 40
- Bread & Butter Pudding with Whiskey & Caramel Sauce, 94
- Sticky Toffee Pudding, 96
- Summer Pudding, 99

R

Rhubarb,
- Rhubarb-orange Chutney, 131
- Rhubarb & Elderflower Crumble, 121

Roasted Beetroot & Citrus Salad with Cashel Blue Cheese, 38

Roasted Cauliflower Steaks, 70

Root Vegetable & Red Lentil Soup, 23

S

Salads,
- Roasted Beetroot & Citrus Salad with Cashel Blue Cheese, 38
- Roasted Cauliflower & Couscous, 71
- Warm Mushroom & Black Pudding Salad, 40

Salmon,
- Chilli-Smoked Salmon Fritters, 44
- Hot Smoked Salmon Chowder, 43
- Pan-Seared Salmon with Dill & Caper Sauce, 68
- Smokehouses, 47

Shepherd's Pie with Cheddar Crust, 56

Sheridans Cheesemongers, 125

Shortbread, 122

Smokehouses,
- Burren, 47
- Connemara, 49
- Gubbeen, 49
- Hederman, 47
- Kinvara, 49
- Ummera, 49
- Woodcock, 49

Soups,
- Hot Smoked Salmon Chowder, 43
- Potato & Celeriac Soup, 19
- Root Vegetable & Red Lentil Soup, 23

Steamed Irish Mussels in Cider Cream, 20

Sticky Toffee Pudding, 96

Summer Pudding, 99

Sweet Chilli Lime Sauce, 45

T

Tarts,
- Buffalo Ricotta & Berry, 102
- Goat Cheese Tarts with Red Onion Marmalade, 34

Three-Cheese Rösti, 86

V

Vegetarian and Vegan, 70

Vinaigrettes,
- Citrus Dressing, 39
- Walnut, 31
- Wholegrain Mustard, 41

W

Walnut & Treacle Bread, 29

Walnut Vinaigrette, 31

Warm Mushroom & Black Pudding Salad, 40

Wholegrain Mustard Vinaigrette, 41

Wild Mushrooms & Ricotta Toast, 33

ST. GEORGE'S MARKET, Belfast, *Tourism Ireland*

THE JOHNSON FAMILY

Bunratty Castle Medieval Banquet, August 1984

For more information about
Margaret M. Johnson
&
Delicious Ireland
please visit

irishcook.com

Margaret M. Johnson
irishcookbook

X @teacrumpet

irish1cook

For more information about
AMBASSADOR INTERNATIONAL
please visit

www.ambassador-international.com
@AmbassadorIntl
www.facebook.com/AmbassadorIntl

www.ingramcontent.com/pod-product-compliance
Lightning Source LLC
Chambersburg PA
CBHW060931180426
43192CB00045B/2889